Władysław Dulęba
Zofia Sokołowska

The Kościuszko Foundation
New York

PWM - Edition
Polskie Wydawnictwo Muzyczne
Cracow

1979

Paderewski

PADEREWSKI

by Władysław Dulęba
   Zofia Sokołowska
Translated from the Polish by Wiktor Litwiński

Volume VII The Library of Polish Studies

General Editor: Eugene Kusielewicz

American Editors: Mary D. Van Starrex
                 Zofia Sywak

Polish Editor: Alina Krehlik

Graphic Design: Adam Młodzianowski

The original Polish version of *Paderewski* was printed in Poland (1976) by the PWM-Edition (Polskie Wydawnictwo Muzyczne) in Cracow, Poland

This revised English edition was made possible through the support of the Friends of Polish Art in Detroit and the American Council of Polish Cultural Clubs, Inc.

Grateful acknowledgement is made to the following for permission to reprint selections in this book:
1. Ignace Jan Paderewski and Mary Lawton, *The Paderewski Memoirs*, 1938. Reprinted by permission from Joseph G. Blum.
2. Rom Landau, *Ignace Paderewski: Musician and Statesman*, 1934. Reprinted by permission from Harper & Row Publishers, Inc.

Library of Congress Catalogue Card No. 78-55893
ISBN 0-917004-14-0

Printed in Poland by Drukarnia Narodowa and Drukarnia Wydawnicza in Cracow.

Table of Contents

In Lieu of a Preface

We got seats on the concert stage... This made us happy on two accounts; first, we would be sitting close enough to watch the pianist's hands and, second, these stage seats, especially requested by him, were priced so as to be within our reach without straining our pockets. I had heard a great deal about Paderewski, chiefly from his three disciples. Sztompka, Dygat and Szpinalski spoke of wonders when talking about their lessons at Riond-Bosson; how exacting, stern and hardworking Paderewski had been, putting a tremendous effort into even the smallest piece that he played, and so on. My chief interest lay with the working routine of such an artist as Paderewski. The fact that a program played on a hundred stages must be practiced afresh after a tour was a critical tenet in Paderewski's work, although little understood by those who assume that having mastered a repertoire an artist is in control of it forever.

The concert in question took place in a lavish building of the Champs Elysées Theater. Strangely enough, the hour was unusual — three in the afternoon, but for some time then Paderewski would play at no other hour. We came to the theater well ahead of time. There were some difficulties in getting seated, for many persons absolutely refused to sit in the first row (there were three rows of chairs onstage). They claimed that they did not want to meet Paderewski's gaze. His habit of keeping his eyes fixed on a person seated close by was supposed to produce an eerie impression. This appeared to me to be slightly exaggerated, so I calmly sat down in the first row right by the keyboard of a superb Erard. The audience thronged. The elite or 'haute monde' as some prefer to call it, sat in the first rows, the tiers farther away from the stage were filled and the balconies were packed, everyone awaiting a great event.

At 3:05 on the dot (one can be five minutes late in Paris) Paderewski comes out, or rather jumps out on stage. He is greeted by a standing ovation. The applause continues until he sits at the piano and starts to improvise. Silence overcomes the hall. Paderewski continues and, without stopping, begins the Handel-Brahms variations. My artistic sensibility is ruffled. How can one switch without interruption from banal roulades and chords into Handel's inspired theme. Meanwhile, Paderewski plays on, indeed superbly, but I do notice faults. The left hand never agrees with the right and outruns it, the fingering technique is hardly superior to the skill of other pianists. What is more, even his touch—which appeared to me to be phenomenal when I had heard him play in a symphonic concert a year before—which fascinated me then, is now gone. I feel somewhat disappointed. It is as if one were pleased to have grounds for criticizing a giant of this caliber while, on the other hand, feeling guilty about detecting some flaws.

More preoccupied with my thoughts than with listening to the music that flows from Paderewski's fingers, I see him turn his head and look straight at me. I bear his gaze awhile. Suddenly I become hot. Paderewski is visibly angry. Am I behaving improperly or have I made a gesture that disturbed his playing? Perhaps he can read one's mind? At any rate I feel very uncomfortable while all these thoughts flash in a fraction of a second. I can no longer endure his gaze. His eyes emanate some sort of fluid whose power I will not be able to oppose. Such must be the eyes of a man in the act of creating, I suddenly realize. I lower my head, ashamed not to have understood it right away...

Now the variations are at an end. The audience is excited. Myself, I am not yet convinced, although I am certainly stunned. During Beethoven's *Sonata* opus 28 the thoughts return obtrusively: why a *ritenuto* like this in a spot where Beethoven never dreamed to put one? I am perplexed by the left hand in constant separation from the right. All of a sudden I hear the piano change its tone. Is it a hallucination? I pinch my hand once and then again. No, I am certainly awake and conscious. The sound of the grand piano dematerializes and ceases to have a piano-like coloring. Only once before did I encounter a similar phenomenon at a concert by Rachmaninoff. With that pianist, this effect resulted from the physiological characteristics of his hand; right from the first a piano chord sounded differently under his fingers, but Paderewski attains his sound only after he gets into his playing.

8 A notable change occurs in me at the same time. I am so overcome by what is happening that I begin to understand how ridiculous I am in being piqued about some *ritenutos* or a *tempo rubato* or even his left hand. I sense that what is transpiring at the moment is by far more important than the technicalities of piano playing. No longer does the preluding before Chopin's *Sonata in b-minor* offend me. From the very beginning the *Sonata* produces a strong impression, but only the *Finale* really reveals what Paderewski is all about. It becomes clear to me that all the criteria of piano playing fail to accommodate Paderewski's scope. I have a distinct feeling that he is not a pianist, but a man who plays the piano, no matter what he does to that instrument, for through his music he is capable of bringing the listener to ecstasy, into some spheres that elude description. I marvel at the pianists who go to watch Paderewski play. I suspect that they leave disappointed. Paderewski plays neither for pianists nor for musicians—he simply plays for people.

He stirs every nerve, every nook of their souls. His conceptions force themselves upon the listeners and appear to be the only acceptable solutions at the moment. A piece he plays serves merely as a pretext to reveal the magic of a great artist. The rather trite and overworked *Hungarian Dance* (No. 6) by Brahms becomes a masterpiece under his fingers for Paderewski is capable of transforming the significance of a musical composition. Striking the first note of Chopin's *Study in a-minor* (opus 25) he put so much pure music into a single sound that I was galvanized with the impression while a young man who sat next to me let out an audible moan. Later, he was unable to explain why he behaved in this manner. Evidently he could not help reacting to the beauty of music coming forth with a single sound. Numerous encores, Debussy among them, conclude the concert. Paderewski bows many times amid the enthusiastic applause of the audience. There is something gallantly Polish in his bow; I am reminded of some characters portrayed by Orłowski. We go to the artist's room where Paderewski is immediately surrounded by a multilingual crowd. The famed Nadia Boulanger, pale and profoundly moved, keeps repeating: "What an artist he is, what an artist". I run into Sviatoslav Stravinsky, the great Igor's son. Uncommonly agitated, the young man reiterates "C'est magnifique, c'est magnifique". In the Polish group, we look at one another and wonder what has just happened to us. We are seemingly the way we were before the concert, but we have been somehow changed by it. Our conversation is unusually spirited as we comment on our impressions and exchange observations. The conversations are interrupted by shouts in the street; Paderewski is leaving in an automobile. The crowds remain in the street for awhile, their eyes follow the slowly moving car.

Tadeusz Szeligowski

Written in 1935 after Paderewski's concert in Paris.

The Early Years

Jan and Polixena (neé Nowicka) Paderewski with their daughter, Antonina

Ignacy Paderewski, the second child of Jan Paderewski, manager of an estate, was born on November 18, 1860 in the village of Kuryłówka, Podolia.

It was one of the most beautiful places in existence. I cannot tell you enough about the country, the softness and freshness of the air, the picturesque, undulating landscape, the soil and the richness of that. And the beautiful fruit! The finest orchards I have ever seen were in the place where I was born.

My mother, from what I know, was a very artistic woman. She had a fine education. She was the daughter of a professor of the University of Wilno, who was an exile himself because he was sent into the interior of Russia by the Russian government after the last war for independence against the Russians in 1830–31, and my mother was born in exile. **13**

My father was everything to us, father and mother both; he was all we had as my mother died soon after my birth. So far as I can remember, he was not very exuberant, but he had a deep sense of humor and was very conscientious and extremely kind to man and beast. My father was administrator of very large estates. He was very artistic in his tastes and had a feeling for all art. He was a painter and a sculptor too, in a modest way... he played the violin. He played very little, just simple tunes, principally dance music for the servants and children to dance to. I did not dance — I have never been fond of dancing, nor has my sister either, but when other children came to our house, and there was a little party there, he was very fond of contributing to it by playing his dance music to add to the gaiety.

Our home was very far from civilization; we were hundreds of miles from the primitive railway station, so that all traveling (and there was very little traveling then) was done by horse, of course.

15

Jan Paderewski and his son, Ignacy

My country was always torn with revolution. My first childish knowledge of it was revolution, and it was in the revolution of 1863 that my father was taken to prison ... He remained there for more than a year. It was this revolution of '63 and '64 which ruined many thousands of people in Poland ...

Whatever he [my father] could do, he did, except that he could not take an active part in the fighting, for that was against his nature.[1]

When Paderewski's father was exiled, the children stayed with their aunt in Nowo-siółki, about 100 kilometers from Kuryłówka.

I was a very lonely boy. My surroundings were so sad and impressed me to such an extent that I became a very melancholy child. I was the only boy in the family — I had no play-mates and my sister was my only companion. We amused ourselves as best we could, but there were not very many resources for amusement under such circumstances. We were very lonely children.

Everything was upset then throughout the Province. The property he [my father] had managed was in receivership. The owners had left, and my father had to look for another position. What a discouragement that must have been for him. But he finally got a new

post in Sudyłków. It was a little township of only about 2,000 population, of which 1,800 were Jews.

It was a sad place to live in, very sad ... Our house stood on a small hill, overlooking a little pond and a large Jewish cemetery. It was frightful — just a few steps from the cemetery ... and at least twice a week I had to see from our little garden the funerals of those poor Jews and hear the laments ... It was really distressing and it went on for hours. Their wails still linger in my ears.

A great change came in our surroundings and this event happened when I was about eight years old. My father married again in 1867, and I acquired a stepmother. There were many brothers and sisters, and life suddenly became quite different.[2]

Michał Babiński, an émigré who returned from exile in France as a result of his participation in the November Insurrection of 1830, took charge of the children's education.

Michael Babiński came in 1868. He had been recommended to my father as a very successful and experienced teacher. With him I had regular lessons in grammar, both in Polish and French, in mathematics, geography, history and so on, just according to my needs and age. He devoted all his time and all his heart to our early education, especially to mine ... His French was perfect and his knowledge of various subjects was very considerable ... It is a fact that I owe to him a great deal of my patriotic feelings, my aspirations.[3]

Paderewski remembered fondly his first music teachers and was quite generous when evaluating their competence. Soon, the children's musical talents became the chief attraction at local charity concerts. At first they played duets, but in 1872 Ignacy performed a solo in two towns, Zasław and Ostróg, which were county seats.

We knew operas by Donizetti and Rossini. We played "Il Barbiere", "Norma", and "Lucia di Lammermoor", but always four-handed, my sister and I, and I always played the bass ... and sometimes our performances were very exciting, especially when we fought

Pecherskaja Lavra
Monastery at Kiev

each other with our elbows, which we generally did very vigorously, accompanied by sudden little kicks as well.

I improvised a good deal, for I did not have access to any musical compositions at that time. I knew only a few things myself. I played some little arrangements from operas that I knew. We were so far away from cities and artistic centers that we did not even have a musical library.

One extraordinary feature of these concerts was that after I had finished my so-called program, someone in the audience, as a great test, came and held a towel over the keyboard, completely hiding the keys, and without seeing them I played again. That was a great effect!

There was one very wealthy family, the family of Count Chodkiewicz, friends of my father's family, who insisted on taking me at this time to Kiev for a few weeks' visit. I was looked upon then as a very talented boy — a promising musician. So they decided to take me to Kiev where I could hear some music ... I had never heard any concerts at that age, nor any music really. I had never heard an orchestra, a pianist, violinist, or even a singer. So this was a great adventure — my first.[4]

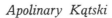
Apolinary Kątski

Gustaw Roguski

At the age of twelve Paderewski left home for Warsaw to obtain a proper musical education. He was accepted by the Musical Institute where he studied theory and the piano with professors J. Śliwiński, R. Strobl, J. Janotha, P. Schölzer, K. Studziński and Gustaw Roguski — the highly-esteemed pupil of Berlioz. Paderewski's relationship with his teachers and especially with the elderly and esteemed director, Apolinary Kątski, were not the best. His musical talents were believed to be far from outstanding and he was expelled for his ornery behavior. Roguski's intervention was only temporary, for again Paderewski came into conflict with the school's authorities and was expelled for a year.

They one and all agreed that I was to be a composer not a pianist ... As it was permitted to every pupil (also encouraged) to join a class of brass, wood and wind instruments, I went ... Well, after having tried to learn so many instruments, and after having acquired a real knowledge — at least theoretically — of their possibilities, I found that it was necessary to study all the others. So I went on to the class of trumpets and of the trombone. Both instruments were under the same teacher, who immediately saw my remarkable talent for both the trumpet and the trombone! One day while giving the lesson, he said, "Now my dear boy, listen to me. You are always trying to play piano. But why? Piano is useless for you — you have no future with the piano. Your future is with the trombone."[5] **25**

The Warsaw Institute of Music

Inspired by youthful enthusiasm Paderewski not quite sixteen, and his violin-ist friend, Roman Cielewicz, who was not much older, set out on a road concert tour of the northern towns of Russia and Poland. They were joined by cellist Michał Biernacki, several years their senior, who soon dropped out of the escapade. The two 'concertanti' continued their tour for nearly a year.

We met with the greatest difficulties, but just when we were in the blackest despair, quite of a sudden would come a little success, which was most unfortunate because we would be so encouraged again, that we would proceed a little further!

Our greatest difficulty always was to find a piano — and very rarely could we find a grand

26

piano anywhere. A small square piano, usually hoarse and of terrible tone and seemingly a hundred years old, was the best we could generally find. Naturally, our first necessity in arriving in a town was to search out the musical people of the place, to whom we immediately paid visits. We would present ourselves in some trepidation and ask to have the use of their piano (if they had one) for our concert that night.

I can say that there was very little time for rest and practice en route. Our entire concert day was spent in finding and then moving the piano. But we were young and it made no difference. The only easy times, I recall, were when we came to a military post, and then the soldiers took a hand. They entered into the spirit of it and were delighted to move the piano for us. But first of all, one of them would try to lift it, and when he found it so terribly heavy, he would begin a great argument that not even four or five men could carry it. Often they would get into quarrels about how many were needed, and sometimes it ended in thirty or forty soldiers coming to carry the piano...[6]

W. Kantor, Z. Trepke, H. Trębicka, R. Szpiro, M. Bogucka

Paderewski received superb grades on his final examinations (1878) and he remained at the Institute as a teacher of piano. Although Warsaw's musical life was rather weak and popularity generally was enjoyed by the established celebrities, Paderewski was recognized as an excellent accompanist and later as a promising composer and pianist. His portfolio already contained such works as *Valse mignonne* (dedicated to Roguski), *Impromptu, Prelude and Capriccio, Minuet in g-minor* and *Trois morceaux* for the piano.

28

And now we come to a great event in my life. I think I shall have to say it very simply —
I fell in love. I was only twenty at that time and in spite of the uncertainty of the future,
I married. I wanted a home, a personal life of my own — a place and some one that
belonged to me.

30 I married in 1880 Antonina Korsak — a young girl who was a student at

the Warsaw Conservatory. I had a little home of my own at last and I was happy —
but it was a short happiness. A year later my wife died, leaving me alone with our child, a
son. I had lived through a brief — a beautiful — experience. Even at twenty, one can
plumb the heights and depths and feel the pain and mystery of life. I now faced another
change — I must go forward alone.[7]

The Great World of Art

Friedrich Kiel   Heinrich Urban

On a year's leave from the Institute, Paderewski leaves Warsaw for Berlin to study composition with an outstanding specialist of contrapuntal forms, Friedrich Kiel, professor at the Royal Academy of Music. In 1883 he left the Warsaw Institute and returned to Berlin to work on instrumentation under the guidance of Heinrich Urban, former pupil of Kiel.

Those days in Berlin were full of new experiences and contacts. Quite a new life opened its doors to me. I was moving forward, a few groping steps at a time, toward the great world — the great world of art.

All kinds of music was to be heard in Berlin. There were plenty of concerts too, too many. Every day many concerts and very good opera. Wagner then was perfectly established and enjoying tremendous popularity and success ... In appearance Berlin was rather theatrical. It was all very military.

Berlin was a city of life and excitement, but little real gaiety. The people did not know at that time how to enjoy themselves, how to amuse themselves.

That was a time of great persecution of the Poles in Germany, and I felt it constantly and deeply. Even in that charming family of my kind publisher, Mr. Bock, I sometimes had to hear very cutting and bitter remarks about my country.

In Mr. Bock's house, which was one of the important ones in Berlin, I had the opportunity of meeting many distinguished artists, chiefly musicians, and there I met all the musical celebrities who were living in Berlin or passing through the German capital.[8]

35

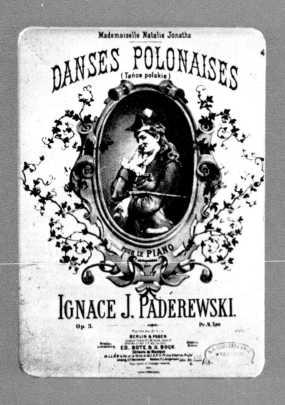

Mademoiselle Natalie Jonatha

DANSES POLONAISES
(Tańce polskie)

POUR LE PIANO

IGNACE J. PADEREWSKI.

Op. 5.   Pr. M 3,00

Propriété des Editeurs
BERLIN & POSEN

ED. BOTE & G. BOCK.
Editeurs de Musique

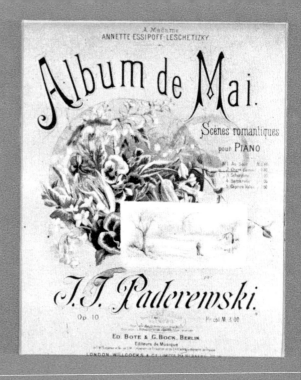

A Madame
ANNETTE ESSIPOFF-LESCHETIZKY

Album de Mai.
Scènes romantiques
pour PIANO

J. J. Paderewski.
Op. 10   Pr. cpl. M. 3,00

ED. BOTE & G. BOCK, BERLIN.
Editeurs de Musique

LONDON WILLCOCKS & Co. LIMITED

Danses polonaises
(Tańce polskie)
pour le PIANO composées par

J. J. PADEREWSKI.

Edition pour Piano à quatre mains.

Op. 5. № 1. KRAKOWIAK (E-dur)
. 2. MAZUREK (E-moll)
. 3. KRAKOWIAK (B-dur)
Pr. complet M 3,50

Op. 9. Cah. I. № 1. KRAKOWIAK (F-dur)
. 2. MAZUREK (A-moll)
. 3. MAZUREK (A-dur)
Pr complet M 3,50

Op. 9. Cah. II. № 4. MAZUREK (B-dur)
. 5. KRAKOWIAK (A-dur)
. 6. POLONAISE (H-dur)
Pr complet M 3,50

Propriété des Editeurs pour tous pays
BERLIN & POSEN

ED. BOTE & G BOCK
Editeurs de Musique

Leipzig, E.F. Steingraber

London, Willcocks & Co 42 Berners Str. W.

Joseph Joachim

Among the celebrities then in Berlin, I must put first the great violinist, Joseph Joachim, who was a noble man and an admirable artist. As an interpreter of classical music, especially of Beethoven, he was absolutely supreme — a highly cultured man in general.

On one occasion, following the suggestion of my publisher ... Joachim invited me to play a few of my own compositions, which of course I did without hesitation. A small collection of short piano pieces published under the title, which I never liked, "Chants du voyageur" was selected for that purpose. The third piece in it (in B-major) seemed to impress Joachim quite particularly — and to such an extent that he asked me to repeat it several times ...[9]

I met Richard Strauss at the house of my publisher, Bock. Sometimes we came in the evening, Strauss and myself ... just to amuse the children we played for them ... dance music. He was not a pianist, but he was chiefly a composer all his life. He turned to conducting later on, but he was always very fond of dance music. He adored it and it was delightful to listen to him. But there was one great drawback to the enjoyment of his playing, and that was also a factor which determined me to study the expression of my own face when playing, namely the awful grimaces Strauss made while at the piano. It was too amusing for words to see, but it was also rather painful. One felt almost embarrassed for him.[10]

Richard Strauss

*There was something a little bit uncanny about him ...
He had a natural greatness in himself — he was a titanic
figure. He was a stormy character — torn by many things.
He was in constant conflict with himself and the necessity
for piano playing, while he was always longing to compose.
That enormous driving power of his, and his ambition too,
drove him on — and on — in his consuming hope for immor-
tality.*[11]

Anton Rubinstein

*... and it was through this intro-
duction of Moszkowski's that
my compositions were published
by Bock.*[12]

Moritz Moszkowski

Pablo de Sarasate

*He was a charming personality and a
marvelous artist, with irreproachable
technique and the most beautiful violin
tone imaginable — more beautiful than
Joachim's. He was not to be compared as
an interpreter, especially of classical
music, with Joachim, but he had much
more charm owing to that exceptionally
beautiful quality of tone.*[13]

Toward the end of his studies with Urban, Paderewski decided to become a pianist.

It was about this time I went for a short vacation to Poland to a place in the Tatra mountains to work on the native music of the peasants, and there I met Madame Modjeska [Modrzejewska], the famous Polish actress. She was still very beautiful. I had seen her before but only on the stage. She was considered the most admirable artist in our dramatic theater.

She was distinguished in every way and had an especially beautiful speaking voice. She had a graceful figure, too, but still there was something in her movements on the stage that perhaps was, shall we say, not so elastic, not so abandoned as Bernhardt, for instance.[14]

There was in Warsaw a very distinguished physician (a genius of a physician), Professor Chałubiński, whom I had met in the mountains. He took a fancy to me because I wrote something about music that pleased him. He was an old man then, about seventy, and I was a youth of twenty-six. He wanted me to come to his house as often as possible, as he was very fond of music. I was not very well at that time, I was rather delicate, always under a strain, but I enjoyed going to his house — there was a certain relaxation and happiness there.[15]

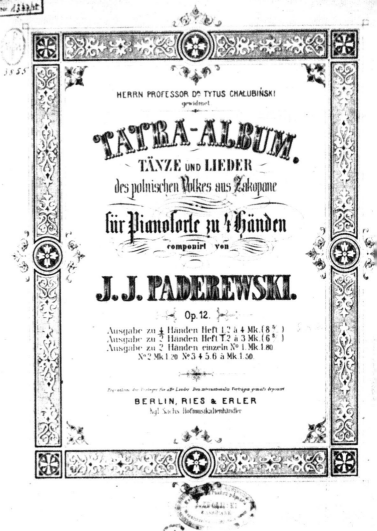

Tytus Chałubiński

In her memoirs the great actress Helena Modrzejewska recalled her first meeting with Paderewski: "Besides the link of personal friendship which binds me to the memory of Dr. Chałubiński, there is yet another: it was in his house and through him that I first met Ignace Paderewski... He used to come often to our villa, and it was impossible to keep him away from the piano. Sometimes he played long after midnight, and had to be taken from the instrument by force when the refreshments were announced. We had many chats, and I advised him to appear in public. I knew he would make a name and fortune. His poetic face, combined with his genius, was bound to produce brilliant results. He hesitated, but finally made up his mind to go to Vienna and study with Leschetizky. That same summer, after leaving Zakopane, he gave a concert in Cracow, at which I had the great pleasure of reciting. Then he departed for Vienna."[16]

Helena Modrzejewska

Cracow, The Market Square

Kraków

Vienna

*Vienna, which is one of the most
beautiful and sympathetic cities on
the Continent, was at that time a very
gay place. It reflected the mood of the
people. There was much splended music, the orchestra, the Philharmonic,
being one of the finest in the world ...
The Vienna Opera, too, was the first
Opera of all the German-speaking
countries. Besides, [Vienna] had the
finest dramatic theatre in the world.
The cycles of Schiller and Shakespeare which were given every year
were really of absolute perfection. They
had a tradition to follow, you see,
and the Court supported all these
theaters very munificently.*

*But the temperament of the Viennese
was quite different, very sympathetic.
There was a great variety in that
population. While the German capital
was purely German, Vienna was a
conglomerate of many nationalities
from which the Austrian Empire was
built. There were Hungarians, there
were Serbs, Bohemians, Slovenes, and
Ruthenians. There were, of course,
a great many Poles, and Poles played
quite an important part in the political administration of the country.*[17]

45

"When in 1886 Paderewski arrived in Vienna to become the pupil of Theodor Le-schetizky, it was not only because the aged Polish musician, after abandoning his career as a pianist, had become the most renowned teacher of his time, but also because no one else would have suited him better. Paderewski's pronounced individualism rendered him antagonistic to any teacher who attempted to impose a method upon him. Practically every music teacher of the time prided himself on having invented a method superior to any other ... Leschetizky had no method; he did not subject his pupils to rules governing their arms, their wrists, their hands, their fingers; the one thing he insisted upon was work, work, and more work ... The result of Leschetiz-ky's methodless method was: 'hardness and a perverse brilliancy'. Leschetizky's insistence upon technical brilliancy saved Paderewski from cheapening the emotional qualities that lay in his playing ... During his time spent with Leschetizky, Pade-rewski also learned another side of piano-playing that was essential to an artist whose ambition was to extend the range of the pianoforte, namely the proper use of the pedal ... In later years this was to be one of the most outstanding features of Paderewski's playing."[18]

Anette Essipoff

Theodor Leschetizky

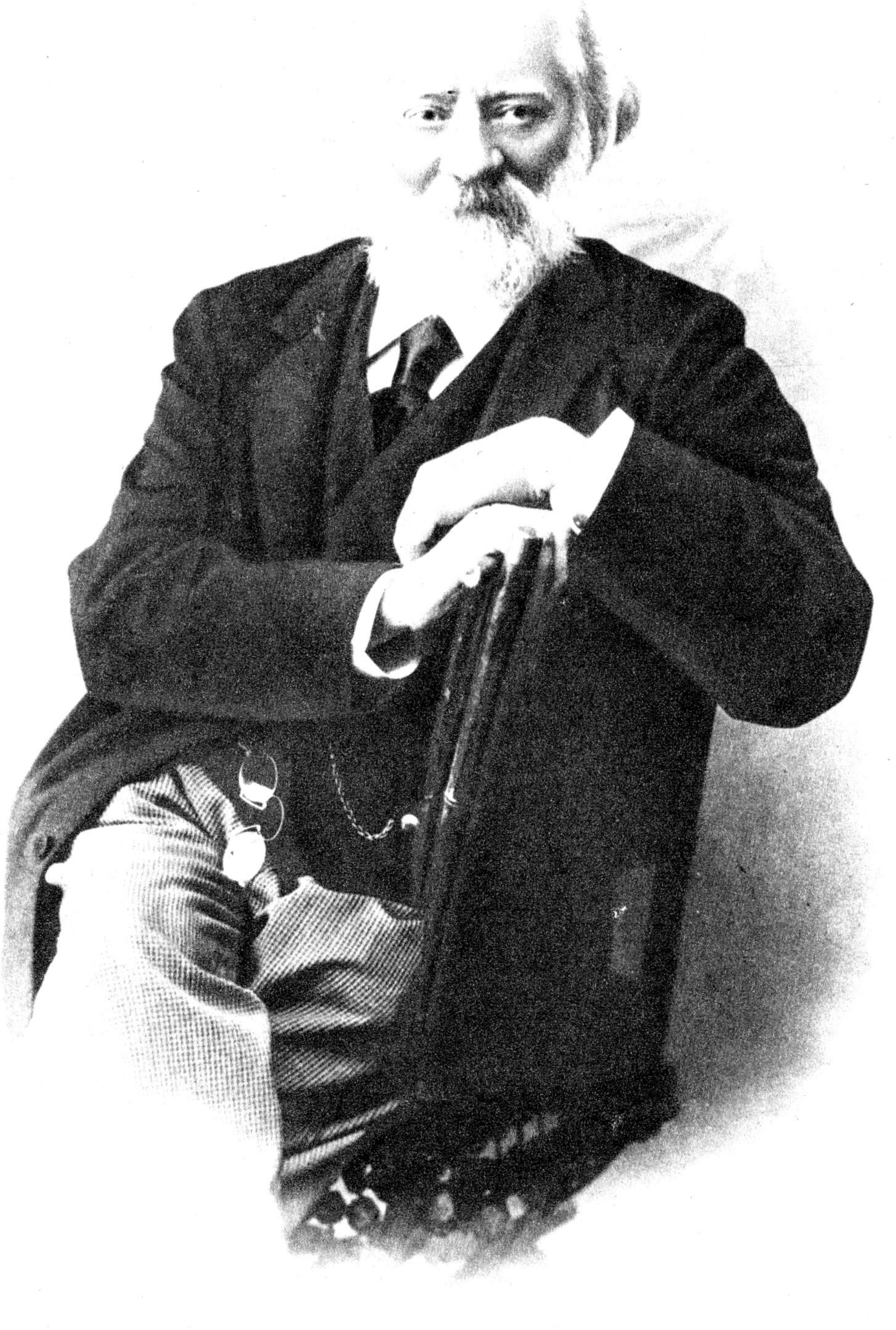

Burlesque, Intermezzo pollaco
et
Cracovienne fantastique
pour Piano

J. J. PADEREWSKI.

À Monsieur
PABLO DE SARASATE

SONATE

pour
Violon et Piano

par
I. J. PADEREWSKI.

M. 6.—

Op. 13

ED. BOTE & G. BOCK, BERLIN W. 8.
Éditeur de Musique
Paris, Max Eschig.

À Madame
Annette Essipoff-Leschetizky.

Dans le Désert.
TABLEAU MUSICAL
en forme d'une
TOCCATA
pour Piano
par
J. J. PADEREWSKI.

Op. 15   Pr. M. 3.00

Propriété des Éditeurs
BERLIN
ED. B...

Compositions
pour
PIANO
par
I. J. PADEREWSKI.

M. 4.— netto

Rbl. 2.40 netto

Dépôt exclusif pour la Russie   Léon Idzikowski, Kieff.

ED. BOTE & G. BOCK, BERLIN. W. 8.
Éditeurs de Musique

Melodie
de

PADEREWSKI.

P. W. M.
Nr. 21035

Brahms in referring to the *Sonata* for the violin and pianoforte wrote: "Well, Paderewski, it is very effective, very fine, but it is not chamber music; it is a concert sonata."[19]

Johannes Brahms

There were two men then reigning alternatively in the field of music. On one side there was a very big camp of Wagnerians, and on the other there were the followers of the old classical masters, who worshipped Brahms. The official musicians, I mean the Academy of Music and all the Conservatories ... were of course all for Brahms. But the public was for Wagner, and the atraction of Wagner was still enhanced by the fact that it was connected with entertainment, that is the opera.

Brahms lived in Vienna and I saw him very often during my stay there. He was unfailingly kind to me. But he was not usually very kind — he had the reputation of being rather brutal at times and he was fond of being brutal — or shall we say brusque — he enjoyed it ...[20]

After these first few months with Leschetizky I felt that I had learnt a great deal, and then just at that moment of accomplishment I was obliged to return to Warsaw again. It was absolutely necessary, as my savings were exhausted and I needed money ... I wrote a violin sonata and a few songs, then I decided to give a concert — my own compositions — in Warsaw, in 1885.

The concert that I'd just given so successfully was not a great help financially. I did not know what to do next — and then suddenly, a few weeks after this, came a little ray of light. I received a letter from Leschetizky telling me that he had heard from the Conservatory in Strasbourg asking him to recommend a professor for that institution.

Leschetizky recommended me very strongly to accept that position which was, to a certain extent, a confirmation of what he had already said about my playing — too late, too late for me ever to become a pianist!

While teaching at the Conservatory the work was very hard, because I had only a few talented pupils.

But the good thing at the Strasbourg Conservatory was my playing in public, difficult as it was. It kept my buried hopes alive ... My playing in public caused me, of course, a great deal of excitement — of suffering too, to put it plainly — but was always rewarded with a positive success. I was progressing.

I was also asked to go to Karlsruhe to play in a concert there. Then I played in some of the small provincial towns of Alsace.[21]

51

In 1886, Paderewski resigned from his post at the conservatory. After his Warsaw friends helped him through his financial difficulties, he returned to Leschetizky.

I composed a few pieces and played them for him, and they pleased him, but they were perhaps a little too heavy for him… Then I played the third piece, the Minuet. That was a revelation to him. "Now this", he said, "is going to be a tremendous success. My wife, Madame Essipoff, must play it in her concerts." And two days later she did play it marvelously well.

One day my practice was interrupted by the arrival of Leschetizky. He began at once and said, "Now I have a suggestion to make to you. Would you not like to make your first appearance here in Vienna? There is an excellent opportunity now. Pauline Lucca (who is a very great singer, a beautiful artist) is giving a charity concert and she wants to have a pianist also, because she cannot fill the whole program …"

It was a very fine concert under fashionable patronage and there was a full house. I played some Beethoven and some Chopin, and some of my own compositions. Although I was absolutely unknown as a pianist on the eve of the concert, I was already looked upon as a personality …

The way seemed open at last, and I determined to hesitate no longer but try at least one recital. So I went to Paris.[22]

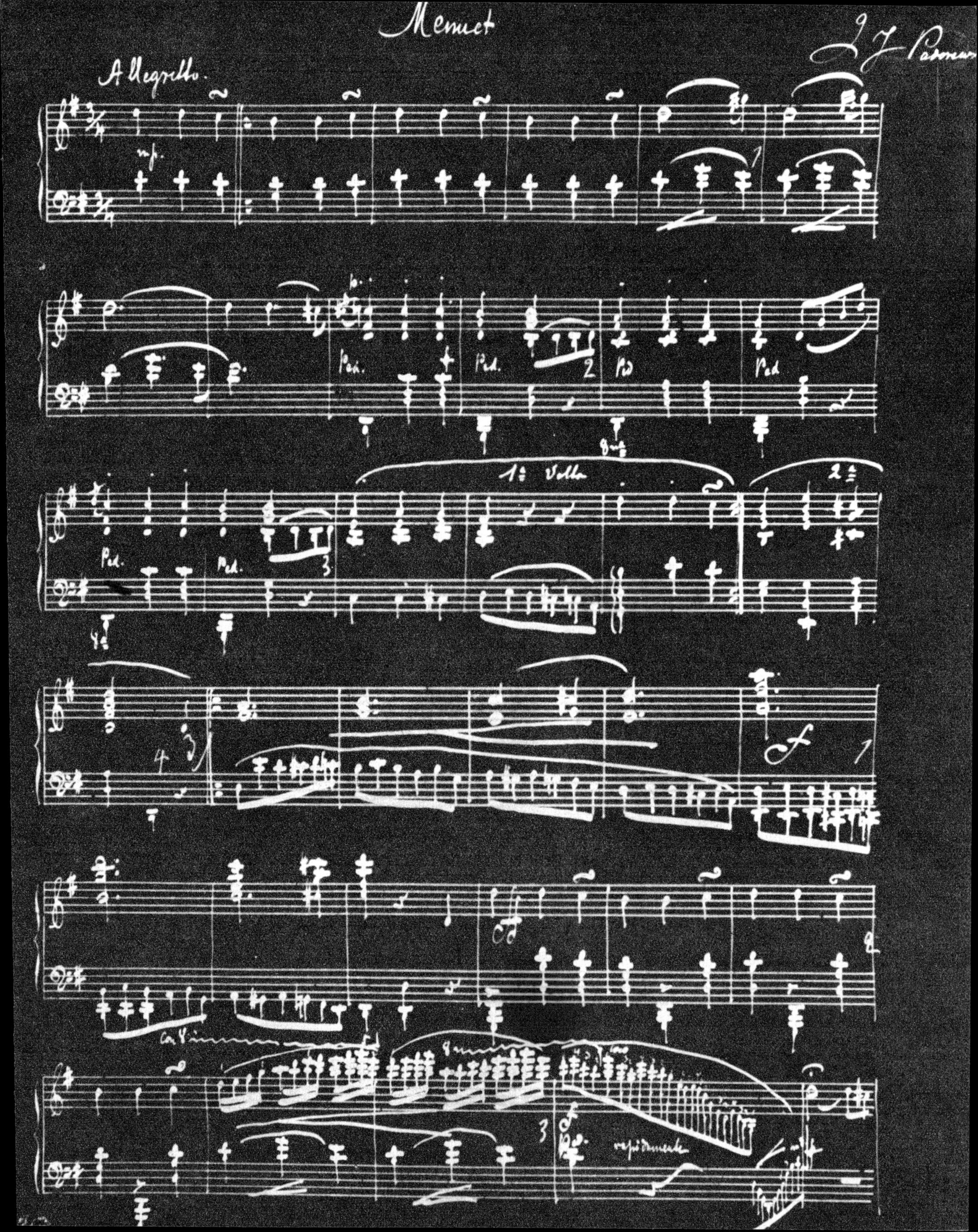

Menuet
Allegretto.
mp.
Ped.
1a Volta
2a
rapidamente

The Lion of Paris

SALLE ÉRARD, 13, rue du Mail

SAMEDI 3 MARS 1888, A 9 HEURES PRÉCISES

CONCERT

DONNÉ PAR M.

J. PADEREWSKI

JEUDI 8 MARS, A 2 HEURES 1/2 PRÉCISES

MATINÉE

Avec le concours de

M*** et de M. GORSKI

PROGRAMME DU CONCERT

1. 32 Variations	BEETHOVEN
2. a. Aria	SCARLATTI
b. Air	HAENDEL
c. Moment Musical	SCHUBERT
3. a. Prélude	
b. Impromptu	
c. Deux Nocturnes	CHOPIN
d. Ballade	
e. Chant Polonais	
4. a.	
b.	PADEREWSKI
c. Cracovienne	
5. a. Étude	
b. Fileuse	LISZT
c. Rhapsodie	

PROGRAMME DE LA MATINÉE
Consacrée aux œuvres de M. PADEREWSKI

1. Sonate pour Piano et Violon (LA mineur)	
2. a. Légende	
b. Mazurka	
c. Chant d'Amour	
d. Scherzino	
e. Variations (N° 2)	
f. Toccata	
3. Chant	
4. a. Sérénade Slave	pour Violon
b. Danse Polonaise	
5. a. Romance	
b. Burlesque	
c. Intermezzo	
d. Cracovienne (N° 3)	

PADE...

PRIX DES PLACES. — Stalles de Parquet (1ers rangs), **20 fr.** — Parquet, **10 fr.** — Première Galerie, **5 fr.**

Billets : Salle ÉRARD et chez MM. DURAND-SCHOENEWERK, 4, place de la Madeleine; FRANDIN, 103, rue Richelieu; HEUGEL, 2 bis, rue Vivienne; GIROD, 16, boulev. Montmartre; GRUS, place COLOMBIER, 6, rue Vivienne; HAMELLE, 22, boulevard Malesherbes; LACOMBE-DUPREZ, 15, faubourg Poissonnière; DURDILLY, 11 bis, boulevard Haussmann.

Paris. — Typographie MORRIS Père et Fils, rue Amelot, 64

M. J. Paderewski, pianiste-compositeur slave, donnera, samedi 3 mars, un concert et, le jeudi 8 mars, une matinée à salle Érard. On dit le plus grand bien de son talent. Le violoni... Gorski lui prêtera son concours.

Albert Blondel

Władysław Górski

The first recital was held on March 3, 1888. Paderewski, the pianist and composer, was sponsored by Mme. Essipoff and Albert Blondel, the director of the famous piano-manufacturers, Erard. Actually his debut as composer occurred five days later at a concert in which his friend, the violinist, Władysław Górski, took part.

It was an extremely brilliant audience. Perhaps one of the reasons for that particularly brilliant audience, so often remarked, was that there was quite a large colony of Polish people in Paris at that time, aristocrats, highly cultured and very musical, and they all attended this concert and brought their friends of the French aristocracy ... Besides the notables already mentioned, there were many prominent French people present, foreigners, and some famous musicians as well. Tchaikovsky, the great Russian composer, who was then in Paris, was there. Then there were the two famous orchestra conductors — Colonne and Lamoureux, and of course Madame Essipoff, and my dear friend, Princess Brancovan, and Madame Trélat, Madame Dubois, the last pupil of Chopin, and so many others. In fact, most of the prominent musicians of the time were there.

The hall was crowded. They were so enthusiastic that I had to play for another hour after the concert. It was all very exciting and I may say it was really a tremendous success. I could hardly believe it — after all my doubts and fears.[23]

During March and April Paderewski gave a few more public concerts and private performances. He signed a contract to appear with the Lamoureux Orchestra and was invited to participate in the various Conservatoire concerts. His career advanced at an astounding pace. At the beginning of the month no one knew even his nationality but by the end of the month he was being hailed as the 'Lion of Paris'.

"Suddenly a strange figure walks across the platform towards the piano, like an exotic bird, with a roseate crest. His flaming crown of hair is of that rarest of colors, a blend of gold and red. The sensitive women in the front rows are not startled by a violent red; they feel the sting of aesthetic enjoyment. All the beauty that flows from under his fingers seems to have been foretold by the rich glow of his hair. Indeed, Monsieur Paderewski corresponds to the romantic ideal which they formed of a pianist from a far country with a picturesque past and with Chopin as its most famous son."[24]

Un pianiste polonais en qui, au dernier banquet de l'Association littéraire internationale, M. Louis Ratisbonne a salué « un Chopin ressuscité », M. Paderewski, donnera, le 26 de ce mois, à la salle Erard, un second concert auquel nous prédisons un succès plus éclatant encore que n'en a eu le premier.

Lundi dernier, la salle Erard a vu un des plus grands succès de la saison. M. Paderewski, le célèbre pianiste, a été acclamé comme compositeur et comme virtuose. C'est sans contredit un des pianistes les plus extraordinaires que nous connaissions. M. Gorski, le violoniste applaudi récemment, a partagé son succès.

It was then that I began to meet many people in all walks of life, important people, and through them I glimpsed another world. I knew all the great musicians of the hour. Their doors opened to me, and Charles Gounod was among the first. His was a wonderful personality. There was something in his appearance which gave you the impression of a High Priest. Gounod was very stately, with a beautiful white beard, wonderfully expressive eyes, and with a facility of speech that was perhaps a little ecclesiastical at times, because it was so unctuous; every sentence was perfect when he spoke — a voice always harmonious and never excessive in intonation. Kind and benevolent in every way, a beautiful man really ... Gounod was not only a composer, but a very learned man. He knew many things, but never wrote about them, as did some of his colleagues. He preferred to write nothing but music ... It was always a joy to me to be with him and it was an added joy for me to see him at my concerts and hear him applauding and shouting his approval ... The next greatest French musician, after Gounod, who became my friend was Camille Saint-Saëns. He was an extraordinary man because he knew so many things. His knowledge was very wide. He wrote philosophical books. He wrote even a book on astronomy ... Saint-Saëns was unfailingly kind to me. He came to my concerts when I played his own
64 *"Concerto in c-minor" and was perfectly enthusiastic ...*[25]

CONCERTS LAMOUREUX

Avant-hier, dernier Concert Lamoureux. Nous y avons entendu un jeune pianiste, M. Paderewski, dans un *concerto* de Saint-Saëns, un *Caprice* et un *Menuet* de sa composition. M. Paderewski est un virtuose de première force, qui en outre nuance fort bien. Son jeu est remarquable à tous les points de vue et on l'a fort applaudi.

CONCERT LAMOUREUX

Les séances sont réservées aux pianistes étrangers. Dimanche dernier nous avons entendu M. Paderewski qui a exécuté un *concerto* de Saint-Saëns puis un *Caprice* et un *menuet* de sa composition.

Ce pianiste possède de grandes qualités ; sa virtuosité est remarquable, son jeu très nuancé et ses compositions ont un certain

que M. Lamoureux a été sur le point de la supprimer. N'oublions pas de signaler, dans cette séance, le nouveau succès remporté par M. Paderewski, le pianiste le plus extraordinaire que l'étranger nous ait envoyé cette année.

Le pianiste russe Paderewski est désormais célèbre. Certes, son talent est indiscutable, et le virtuose se tire avec une aisance extraordinaire des plus grandes difficultés. Dirons-nous cependant que sa qualité de son est loin d'égaler celle de notre regretté Ritter? Comme il se faisait mieux entendre en cette même salle du cirque du boulevard des Filles-du-Calvaire !

L'Enchantement du Vendredi-Saint de *Par-*

Paderewski had not anticipated such a tremendous success. However, due to his limited repertoire, he returned to Leschetizky and prepared for his artistic career. Meanwhile Mme. Essipoff promoted his first major composition — *Concerto in a-minor.*

Then came another great event for me — I had a real debut in Vienna, in 1889, and that was an immense, immediate success. It was my first recital in Vienna. It took place in the Bösendorfer Hall. Bösendorfer was a famous piano maker in Vienna and he had a very large concert hall in his piano house. [He] was a charming gentleman, very friendly with artists, and he treated me with special kindness and cordiality. That concert attracted a very large audience, and I even then in Vienna made quite a nice little sum of money with my recital. The critics of Vienna received me with great enthusiasm. Here is perhaps the moment that I may say they hailed me as 'a great star'. My career as a pianist was then launched.[26]

HANS v. BÜLOW.

Hans Richter   Hans von Bülow

It was an age of great conductors and I had the rare good fortune of meeting many of
them.

Well, one of the most popular was Hans von Bülow, who was extremely erratic in everything, and so he was in his career. His performances were sensational, but they were
perfect in every way ... In speaking of von Bülow one always thinks of his connection
with Liszt and the effects of his marriage to Liszt's daughter, Cosima. It is a long story,
and had we might say, great importance and publicity at the time — and still has for
some people. Cosima was married to von Bülow, and after some years left him and married
Wagner.

... Richter was among the most eminent and finest interpreters of Wagner, and not only
of Wagner, but of all classical music. He never tried to make extraordinary effects and
give sensational readings of Beethoven and the other Masters. He just gave a solid,
sound and yet refined performance of every work he conducted.[27]

68

Vienna

Antwerp

Bruxel[...]

Paderewski

Brussels

After that debut in Vienna, my real debut as I always call it, I felt my career had already begun and I was fully prepared now to give three programs in Paris, the result of my final work with Leschetizky. So I returned to Paris at once, ready and eager.

It was at the time of the Exhibition in 1889 and I was asked to give a concert at the Exhibition, which I gladly did.

I was then getting many engagements. My reputation was growing more and more. I played many times in Brussels, Liège, Antwerp and so on, and then in the provincial towns of France. I played in Lyons, Bordeaux, and Nantes, and also several times in Nancy, concerts and chamber music.

... at Tours, first some one sang, a baritone I think, and then I had to play. I played, and the audience was very much pleased, and I was glad, though I did not expect much enthusiasm there. Then a lady singer sang. Then came Galipaux. He was an actor of great talent, and very popular then. He recited one of his amusing monologues, and he absolutely changed the atmosphere. Next came a tenor. He was rather a mediocre singer, but he had the most marvelous high notes. Those top notes of his sent his audience quite crazy with delight ... I had to play after him! Then came Galipaux, the actor — another success and then the tenor — the tenor with the top notes. This time he was simply a furore. The audience went wild! So wild that when I appeared right after his number, to play my last group of solos, well, this time nobody listened to me at all — they simply began talking. They paid no attention to me whatever. I thanked God when it was finished.[28]

73

London

During his first English tour in May 1890, Paderewski was initially received rather coolly in London. His first recital was almost a flop.

[George Bernard] Shaw's criticism, or perhaps I might say, his attack upon me was almost as violent as he declared my attack was upon the piano! It was his criticism of my first concert and he said among other devastating things that I was a harmonious blacksmith who laid a concerto on the piano as upon an anvil, and hammered it out with exuberant enjoyment — words not easily forgotten![29]

George Bernard Shaw wrote to Mary Lawton. "... I am glad to find that I made no mistake about him. He appears in my notices as the greatest pianist of that time, and probably of all time. He has forgotten them all except one which annoyed him ... there had been a change in the instrument. The old wooden pianos which made fame of Broadwoods, and for which Beethoven and Chopin composed, had been supplanted by a monster called the iron grand, now a steel one. Leschetizky, the greatest teacher of that day, realized that a steel piano needed steel fingers to play it. He taught Paderewski a touch undreamt of by Wieck or Kullak ... Paderewski did not know that this was a novelty in London."[30]

ST. JAMES'S HALL.

MONS.

PADEREWSKI'S

FIRST

✶ Pianoforte ✶ Recital, ✶

FRIDAY AFTERNOON, MAY 9, 1890,

AT THREE O'CLOCK.

❖ Programme. ❖

No. 1.—*a.* PRÉLUDE ET FUGUE	... ...	MENDELSSOHN
b. AIR VARIÉ	... ...	HAENDEL.
„ 2.—FANTAISIE (Op. 17)		SCHUMANN.
„ 3.—*a.* TROIS ETUDES		
b. NOCTURNE		
c. MAZURKA	... ...	CHOPIN.
d. VALSE		
„ 4.—TROIS HUMORESQUES À L'ANTIQUE :		
a. CAPRICE		
b. SARABANDE	... ...	PADEREWSKI
c. MENUET		
„ 5.—*a.* BARCAROLLE		RUBINSTEIN.
b. RAPSODIE		LISZT.

Dates of the remaining Recitals—MAY 20, MAY 29, and JUNE 6, 1890.

Stalls and Balcony (Reserved), 7/6.　Balcony (Unreserved), 3/-
Admission One Shilling.

It was at Lady Barrington's house too that I met Henry James many times — the famous American author who was a notable figure in the literary world of London. I liked Henry James immensely from the moment I met him, but there was something that always appeared a bit artificial in his speech. Whether he spoke English, which he spoke beautifully, or French — and his French was perfect — there was something a little too academic for intimate conversation.

Among the many outstanding figures in the musical world of London there was a remarkably gifted man — a good conductor, a brilliant accompanist and a fine teacher, whose chief occupation, however, was singing. His name was Georg Henschel. With the mere shadow of a voice, an ugly, small voice in fact, he could produce the greatest emotional effects.

It was in 1891 that Queen Victoria had expressed a desire to hear me play. I think I have already told you that she made a very deep impression upon me then ... So I went to Windsor. It was really an admirable evening. It happened that the Queen was not feeling very well, so she arrived in the hall in an invalid chair. She addressed me in beautiful French and impressed me as being a queen in every sense of that often misused word ... I was surprised to find that she knew so much about music. She had studied among other things, the piano and was said to be one of the few pupils of Mendelssohn — such is the legend — so her favorite composers were either before or during the period of Mendelssohn's life.[31]

CONCERTS

M. Paderewski gave an extra recital on Saturday, when St.
James's Hall was more densely crowded than it has been at a
recital since M. Rubinstein last appeared. The programme was
devoted exclusively to the works of Chopin, in which the young
Polish pianist 'excels. "The Funeral March" Sonata, the well-
known valse in D flat, which was given for an encore, and again
repeated, and The Berçeuse were amongst the most successful items of a programme which comprised altogether twenty-
one pieces. Miss Liza Lehmann, the popular young singer, has
also given a successful vocal recital. At the last of the Richter
Concerts on Monday Madame Von Arnhem, a dramatic soprano
with a fine voice, which, however, seems a little worn, sang
Beethoven's Concert aria, "Ah, Perfido," and Grieg's *Peer Gynt*
suite, which is thoroughly well-known elsewhere, was performed for
the first time at these concerts.

M. Paderewski's "Chopin Recital" at St. James's Hall
on Saturday afternoon attracted probably the largest, and
certainly the most enthusiastic audience that has been seen
at any pianoforte recital since Rubinstein left us. Doubtless
the popularity of the pieces selected, as much as their masterly
renderings, contributed in great degree to the presence of
the latter element, but M. Paderewski's playing is permeated
with a strong national individuality, always a powerful
attraction, and in no works is this individuality so prominent
as in those by Chopin. It is not the Chopin we have been
accustomed to hear; where the composer has marked *giusto*,
we are often given gentle and capricious waywardness, and
expected *forte* passages are sometimes played *piano*; but it
is a Chopin which in turn fascinates by its exquisite delicacy
and refinement and outbursts of wild passion. To some,
courtesy would seem to take the place of tenderness, and the
passionate brilliancy to have a ring of cruelty, but when a
Pole is interpreted by so talented a countryman, it would be
hazardous to dogmatize as to which was the correct reading.
However it be, such were the characteristics which marked
the renderings of the "Fantasia in F minor," the "Sonata in
B flat minor," and sixteen other pieces, every class of Chopin's
compositions being represented. The "Etude in G flat," op.
25. No. 9, was repeated, and the "Valse in D flat" given
twice as encores. Three additional pieces were also played
at the close of the performance, amidst one of the wildest
scenes of enthusiasm that has ever taken place in St. James's
Hall.

He posed for portraits by the famous English pre-Raphaelites, Edward Burne-Jones and Lawrence Alma-Tadema, and for the sculptor, Albert Gilbert. His portrait was also painted by Queen Victoria's daughter, Louise, who later became Princess d'Argyll. The day after Burne-Jones made his initial sketch of Paderewski, he described Paderewski to a friend in the following manner: "There's a beautiful fellow in London named Paderewski and I want to have a face like him, and look like him and can't ... there's trouble. He looks so like Swinburne looked at twenty that I could cry over past things, and the pretty ways of him ... courteous little tricks ... and low bows and a hand that clings in shaking hands, and doesn't want to go ... and a face like Sir Galahad, and the Archangel Gabriel ... very like Swinburne's only in better drawing, and little turns and looks so like that it makes me jump ... and knowing people say he is a great master of his art ... which might well be for he looks glorious. I praised Allah for making him ... how nice it must be to look as fine as one is inside."[32]

By Edward Burne-Jones

By Lawrence Alma-Tadema

By Louise d'Argyll

America Discovered

At the end of 1891, Paderewski left for America. His concerts were sponsored by House of Steinway, the well-known American manufacturers of pianos, in return for which Paderewski agreed to use only their pianos in the United States.

When I finally landed in New York, New York was far from being that land of mountains and shooting towers illuminated so brilliantly and making such an over-whelming impression as now. There were only small, dirty, low buildings near the wharf in those days.

...I was suffering too much. The pain in my right hand and arm was increasing. There was a reason for this. Steinway pianos, universally recognized as the most marvelous instruments in the world, had a certain peculiarity which was rather dangerous for concert players. Their action at that time was extremely heavy and fatiguing. I realized this must be changed. The Steinways were willing to do everything in their power to comply with my wishes, but their workmen ... were the decided enemies of any change or any innovation ... But finally I had my way ...[33]

Paderewski's difficulties were compounded by the demanding conditions imposed on him by Steinway: during the first week three orchestral performances in New York, the programs of which included besides piano concertos (at that time Paderewski's repertoire included Chopin's *Concerto in e-minor* and Rubinstein's *Concerto in d-minor*) a number of solo pieces. The following week consisted of six recitals. Despite this strenuous schedule, the first concert with Walter Damrosch was a preview of the spectacular career that would follow. The music critic for the 'New York Herald' wrote: "Among the many debuts by pianists, which the present generation undoubtedly considers both as musical feasts as well as sensational events, one can list Rubinstein's first concert in 1872, Bülow's (which took place several years later) and d'Albert's debut two years ago. Now to this list can be added the name of Paderewski who played in America for the first time last night. He scored a success which could inebriate any artist in his place".

Following New York city (the first performance was held on November 17, 1891) he was hailed in Boston, Chicago, Philadelphia, New Orleans, San Francisco and other places. The tour lasted six months and consisted of 120 concerts and recitals. America was conquered.

"Before the century was over, Paderewski was to the American mind the virtuoso incarnate, as the novelists depicted and the masses imagined him... In America, it was his very success that appealed to the public imagination: success and the expression of success, which made the most convincing criterion ... His name was popular enough to make Paderewski candies and Paderewski soap pay irrespective of their quality. Children were given for Christmas toys representing a little man with a black frock coat, a white bow tie and a huge head of flame-colored hair, sitting at a piano; when a screw was turned on the little man's hands rushed up and down the keyboard and his head shook violently ..."[34]

Life has a way of repeating itself, and in America, as in London and Paris, every one was very kind to me, and I was immensely struck then, and I still am, with the constant hospitality and friendly feeling of the American people. I was everywhere received with touching evidences of their interest and friendship. The whole American 'scene' ... was of a vitality and freshness unlike anything I had ever known. The names of hundreds of interested and kindly people flock to my mind — charming acquaintances interested in my career, and all a part of the audiences that I found to welcome me throughout the land.[35]

Chicago

New Orleans

San Francisco

Boston

1 szt. Gammy, skrady –
hext, oktawами 7 dur, A mol
Rapsodja – Valse.

{ 2. Koncert
{ 3 Fantazja
      Koncert

{ 4 Sonaty I.
{ 5 Rapsodje – polonез

_____

     Fugi na osjedi
3) Koncert
Fantazja   Polonez
Francuzy ... Scarlatti

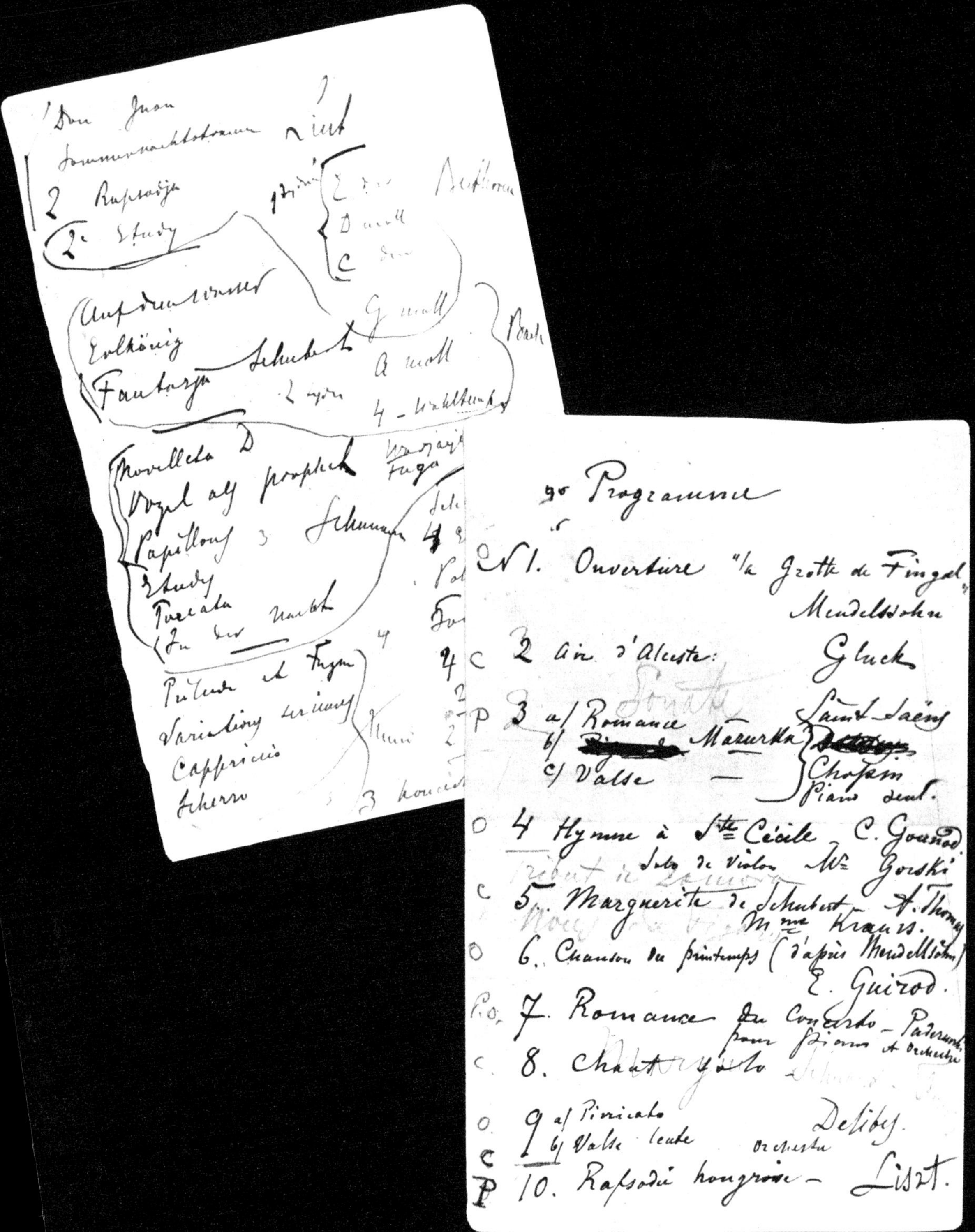

Handwritten notes (two overlapping cards).

Card 1 (upper left):

Don Juan
Sommernachtstraum — Liszt
2 Rhapsodie
2e Study

Es dur — Beethoven
D moll
C dur

Aufforderung
Erlkönig — Schubert
Fantasie
G moll
A moll
4 — Hexenbraut(?)

Novelletta
Vogel als prophet
Papillons
Study
Toccata
(In der Nacht
Prelude et Fuge
Variationen serieuses
Cappricio
Scherzo

Fuga
Schumann

Card 2 (lower right):

2º Programme

N 1. Ouverture "la Grotte de Fingal"
          Mendelssohn

C 2 Air d'Alceste — Gluck

P 3 a/ Romance
   b/ Mazurka — Saint-Saëns
   c/ Valse — Chopin
          Piano seul.

O 4 Hymne à Ste Cécile — C. Gounod
       Solo de violon — Mr Gorski

C 5 Marguerite de Schubert — A. Thomas
       Mme Krauss.

O 6 Chanson du printemps (d'après Mendelssohn)
       E. Guirod.

P.O. 7 Romance du Concerto — Paderewski
       pour piano et orchestre

C 8 Chant...

O 9 a/ Pizzicato
   b/ Valse lente — Delibes.
       orchestre

C P 10. Rapsodie hongroise — Liszt.

After this exhausting American tour Paderewski returned to Europe. Financial problems forced him to continue performing despite the fact that his hand kept bothering him. He prepared for a second American tour. This time he stayed longer in Chicago and gave concerts with the Chicago Symphony, under the directorship of Theodore Thomas, at the World's Fair in May of 1893.

Antonina Paderewska

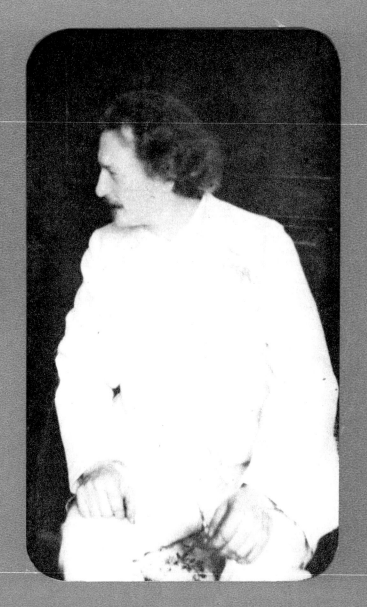

Aix-les-Bains

That summer, physically exhausted and close to a mental breakdown, Paderewski vacationed in Yport, Normandy. He was accompanied by his son, who lived with the Górskis, and by his sister and a few close friends. He resumed composing and soon completed the *Polish Fantasy* for piano and orchestra. Its première occurred in that same year at a festival in Norwich. Due to the persisting pain in his hand even after he stopped giving concerts, Paderewski left for Aix-les-Bains, a health resort in the Savoy Alps.

Sześć Pieśni

do słów

Adama Mickiewicza

muzykę napisał

J. J. Paderewski.

Op. 18.   Cena M. 5.__

Własność wydawnicza na wszystkie kraje

BERLIN i POZNAŃ

Nakładem dostawcy muzykaliów
Lipsk: E.F.Steinacker.

EDWARD SCHUBERTH & CO.   WESSEL & CO Limited
New York.   LONDON. W.

À Madame la Princesse
R. Bassaraba de Brancovan.

Fantaisie Polonaise

sur des thêmes originaux

pour

Piano et Orchestre

par

I. J. PADEREWSKI.

Op. 19

Partition pour Piano et Orchestre	M 18.__
Parties d'Orchestre	M 25.__
Parties du Quatuor separées chaque	M 2.__
Partition pour deux Pianos par l'auteur	M 10.__

Majoration

ED. BOTE & G. BOCK
BERLIN W.8   Fondé en 1838

Amsterdam

Dresden

His rest period was not long. This time concert tours took him to England and Ireland. In London, Paderewski performed his *Fantasy* and accompanied Edward Lloyd in his *Six Songs*. He also gave concerts in Dublin, Belfast and Cork. The following years until 1897 were filled with concert tours in Europe and America. His American tours spanned the entire United States from the Atlantic to the Pacific.

93

Repertuar Paderewskiego.

Program trzech audycyj warszawskich jest tak obfity, że istotnie trudno zrozumieć że ogrom tych koncertów i sztuk w szerokich zarysach odegra jeden artysta. Oprócz olbrzymiej organizacyi muzycznej, potrzeba na to wytrzymałości nerwowej i muskularnej, do której ten mistrz pracy i wytrwałości doszedł drogą trudów usilnych a metodycznych.

Dochód ze sprzedaży programów będzie przeznaczony na cele dobroczynne, mianowicie z koncertu pierwszego na wpisy dla uczniów, z drugiego na szpital dziecięcy, z trzeciego na przytułki noclegowe. Nie chcąc więc uszczuplać dochodu tym celom, ograniczamy się dziś na podaniu programu *pierwszego* koncertu, d. 15 b. m. o godz. 1 w południe w sali Ratuszowej.

1. Uwertura *Eleonora* Beethovena wykona orkiestra teatru Wielkiego pod dyrekcyą Emila Młynarskiego.

2. *Koncert* Schumanna—Paderewski z orkiestrą.

3. *Koncert f-mol* Chopina — Paderewski z orkiestrą.

4. *Koncert es dur* Beethovena (op. 73)—Paderewski solo.

5. *Fantazya* polska—Paderewskiego, wyk. kompozytor z orkiestrą.

Cele dobroczynne, na rzecz których mistrz przeznacza całkowity dochód z trzech koncertów oznaczone będą przez niego samego później.

In 1899, on his way to tour Russia, Paderewski made a brief visit to Warsaw. He gave a number of charity concerts, appearing for the first time in the capital since his conservatory days and was received with enthusiasm.

He visited his dear old friends, the Kerntopfs, for whom — especially Edward — he had a sincere fondness. As an expression of his affection, Paderewski gave concerts in Warsaw, Odessa and Kiev on pianos made by the Kerntopf firm.

ORCHESTRE SYMPHONIQUE
de la Cour IMPERIAL

13 Fevrier 1899.

1. Ouv. de la trag. «Coriolan» op. 62 . .   Beethoven.
2. Prémier concert pour piano avec accompagnement d'orchestre. . . . .   Liszt.
        Exécuté par M-r I. **Paderewski**.
3. a) «Harpe éolienne» du monodrame «Lélio»   Berlioz.
    b) Marionnettes des scènes de ballet . .   Glazounow.
4. Troisieme concert-op. 61, pour violon avec accompagnement d'orchestre . . . . .   Saint-Saëns.
        Exécuté par M-r H. **Marteau**.

Entre'acte.

5. Prélude du drame lyrique «Werther» .   Massenet
6. Solo de piano . . . .   *,*
        Exécuté par M-r I. **Paderewski**.
7. Canzonette de la suite symphonique .   Gardin.
8. Solo de violon: a) Romance . . . . .   Sinding.
        b) Polonaise (en ré). .   Wieniawsky.
        Exécuté par M-r H. **Marteau**.
        Accompagné par M-r A. **Wullus**.
9. Marche française de la Suite Algérienne .   Saint-Saëns.

St. Petersburg

A Soirée at the Home of Stassov

His concerts in St. Petersburg were received warmly by both the press and the public. Only the conservatory, faithful to the memory of its founder, Anton Rubinstein, failed to receive him warmly. In Moscow, he performed his own *Fantasy* under the direction of Vassily Safonov.

97

At Home

Paderewski's Home at Riond-Bosson

He visited Warsaw again in May 1899, on strictly personal business: to marry Helena Górska, née Rosen. They departed for Riond-Bosson, a newly-acquired estate on Lake Geneva.

When my poor boy was so ill, almost helpless in fact, after much experimenting and being taken from one grandparent to another, he was finally put under the care of the Górski family, friends of mine from student days ... But it was Madame Górska who took care of my son ; she cared for him during all those years like a mother. He became attached to her naturally and was thankful for her attention and her care altogether ... At that time the Górskis lived in Paris and I was a frequent guest at their house. I saw my son every day during my Paris sojourns and I cannot deny that I was very much touched and also attracted by Madame Górska. And that attachment developed into love. I can only say it like that, very simply. Górski himself saw and realized this and was the first to ask for the divorce. It was a difficult time for every one, a time of tension and emotion ...[36]

—a— **J. I. Paderewski** zaślubił w Warszawie d. 31 maja w kościele św. Ducha panią Helenę z Rozenów Górską. Znakomity artysta bawił w Warszawie przez dni pięć, poczem państwo Paderewscy udali się do majątku swego Rozprza, zkąd resztę lata przepędzą w wilii pod Lozanną w Szwajcarii.

—a— **P. Oktawjusz Nouwelli,** profesor klasy śpiewu solowego w konserwatoryum warszawskiem napisał broszurę p. t. *La Respiration et l'emission du son vocal chez les grands chanteurs de*

ECHO

MUZYCZNE, TEATRALNE I ARTYSTYCZNE.

Nr. 36 (779.) Warszawa,
dnia 22 Sierpnia (3 Września) 1898 r.

Konkurs Muzyczny
imienia
J. I. PADEREWSKIEGO.

HENRYK MELCER
(nagroda za koncert fortepianowy).

EMIL MŁYNARSKI
(nagroda za koncert skrzypcowy).

ZYGMUNT STOJOWSKI
(nagroda za symfonię).

GRZEGORZ FITELBERG
(nagroda za sonatę na skrzypce i

Konkurs imienia Paderewskiego.

W dniu 1-ym b. m. upłynął ostateczny termin do nadsyłania pod adresem redacyi *Bibljoteki warszawskiej* utworów na konkurs dramatyczny imienia Paderewskiego.

Obecnie od redakcyi tegoż miesięcznika, w uzupełnieniu poprzednio ogłoszonych dwóch wykazów dzieł dawniej nadesłanych, otrzymujemy zawiadomienie, że do powyżej oznaczonego terminu złożono jeszcze 50 utworów, z zaznaczeniem, iż wykazy poprzednie kończyły się na numerze 29-ym.

Oto trzecia i ostatnia lista nadesłanych utworów:

30) „Ku lepszemu", dramat w 5-iu aktach, godło: „Ora et labora."

31) „Koledzy". komedya w 3-ch aktach z prologiem, godło: „Miej serce i patrzaj w serce."

32) „Samotnik". obraz dram___ __y w 4-ch aktach. godło: „Nie masz wrog___ ___"

__) ___ ___? sztu___ ___n.
8___

During his third American tour in 1896, Paderewski funded a competition for young composers. He set aside $10,000, a sizeable sum even by American standards at that time, the interest from which was devoted to triennial prizes to best compositions. Zygmunt Stojowski, Henryk Melcer and Grzegorz Fitelberg were winners in the first competition. In 1899 Paderewski, accompanied by his wife, set out on his fourth American tour which also included Mexico. That same year Paderewski created a fund for playwrights, with Lucjan Rydel and Józefat Nowiński being its first winners. **103**

Manru.

Oper in drei Aufzügen.

Dichtung von **Alfred Nossig**.

Musik
von

J. J. Paderewski.

Vollständiger Klavier-Auszug mit deutschem Text
bearbeitet von F. H. Schneider.
M.20. netto

Ed. Bote & G. Bock, Berlin.
Hofmusikalienhandler.

... a Polish writer and poet, Alfred Nossig by name, had approached me repeatedly with a proposition for writing a book for an opera. So, out of the several outlines suggested, I selected one which was afterwards written for me. That book, though not then in its definite form, was sent me toward the end of 1893, and became the libretto for my opera "Manru".

... in that year, 1897 ... I went on to revise my sketch of the opera, and introduced some changes in the libretto to make the action a bit more lively and dramatic, and consequently had to write many new songs and change a great deal of the musical text.

... On the whole, about two and a half years were spent working on it. I could not write continuously and there were intervals in which I was entirely out of the mood of the composition, but I finally did succeed in scoring the first act. Everything stopped then because I had already arranged for a tour in Russia in 1899. That was my first tour there since the youthful disaster twenty years before.

...My opera was still unfinished and calling me. I was in a great hurry to go on with the work and I started the orchestration. I must say that rarely did I do any work with greater interest and pleasure. Whatever may be the shortcomings of that opera, those of which I know and those of which I am completely ignorant, I am thankful to say that the orchestration, even when I look back at it after so many years, gives me complete satisfaction. I finished it in January, 1901.[37]

The world première of *Manru*, conducted by the renowned Ernst von Schuch, was held on May 29, 1901 at the Royal Opera in Dresden. Among the guests were celebrities along with Paderewski's personal friends, including Leschetizky and Joachim. Having seen *Manru* that summer, Mme. Sembrich-Kochańska and Maurice Grau, director of the New York Metropolitan Opera, decided to stage it the following season in New York.

Ten days after the Dresden première, *Manru* was staged at the Lvov Opera with the world-renowned Bandrowski in the principal role. The composer was greeted with standing ovations. Next the Lvov Opera Company presented *Manru* in Cracow, and the following season it was staged at the Great Theater in Warsaw, and again in 1904. Antoni Sygietyński wrote of this performance:

"To the public's delight, Paderewski was in his box and the complete opera was performed, with exactly the same results it enjoyed a few years before, that is, no substantial success during the performance nor after it. This comes as no surprise since the opera is a hodgepodge. First of all the story is neither interesting nor amusing. Kraszewski in his *Chata za wsią* gave vent to the sentimentality which was, at that time, a good

The Opera House in Lvov

Aleksander Bandrowski in the principal role, Manru

expression of the general poetic mood. Galasiewicz and Zofia Meller in their adaptation created a melodrama full of emotional scenes. Nossig, the author of the libretto, in his adaptation created a tableau with no plot, no psychological drama, no poetry ... Paderewski whose creative output includes quite a few nice, though not exclusively original, pieces, this time failed to think through, to compose, create, expel from his soul, which does not lack in diverse poetic wealth, some kind of all inclusive emotion ... Ultimately Paderewski's opera is valuable, original, unusual and modern not because of its originality and independence of emotion or unique temperament, but purely as a kaleidoscopic instrumental piece. In fact, each performance of *Manru* should be regarded not as a staging of a lyrical drama, for there is none, but as a lesson in instrumentation."[38]

The Metropolitan Opera House
in New York

During the 1902 concert season, Paderewski conquers New York city. Simultaneously, while he was giving a recital at Carnegie Hall, *Manru* was being performed at the Metropolitan Opera House.

The first performance was extremely well received. Madame Sembrich was quite marvelous and Bandrowski excellent. Walter Damrosch conducted, and very well indeed ... For reasons I fail to understand, "Manru" was not maintained in the Metropolitan repertoire, though five or six performances were crowded. It was given in New York, Chicago, Baltimore, Philadelphia, Boston, and Pittsburgh. It was performed in Europe — in Cologne, Bonn, Prague, Zurich, Warsaw where it had a very great success, and in Kiev.[39]

"There was in fact so much trite drawing of analogies amongst the critics that Paderewski felt compelled to state in an interview his attitude towards operatic composition in general ... 'In music absolute originality does not exist, it is the temperament of the composer that makes his work. In method one cannot help but follow those who have gone before. When a great genius like Wagner introduces a method that will give better expression to an idea, it is not only a sin not to follow it, but it is a duty to follow it ...' "[40]

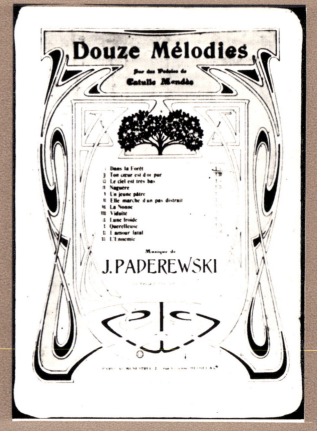

... *in 1903 I remained almost the entire year at Morges, and began to compose. First of all I wrote my "Piano Sonata", which is one of my most important and best works. But it is extremely difficult and for that reason will never be very popular. The second work was the completion of my third set of "Variations", which I had begun years before while still in Strasbourg. I had retained only a few of the variations from that period, so I wrote a series of new ones ending with the fugue. This work is my best piano composition, I think. It is extremely difficult and perhaps too long, but it contains quite a few things which were then almost a revelation in their character and novelty. Within a fortnight I also wrote twelve French songs to the words of Catulle Mendès. Madame Modjeska and her husband were staying here at Morges then, and every evening I played a new song to her. It was a happy time. After that I wrote a sketch of my Symphony. That took several months. The orchestration, however, was done several years later. That composition was written in commemoration of the last Polish revolution of 1863. It was the fortieth anniversary.*[41]

Paderewski's Work-Study at Riond-Bosson

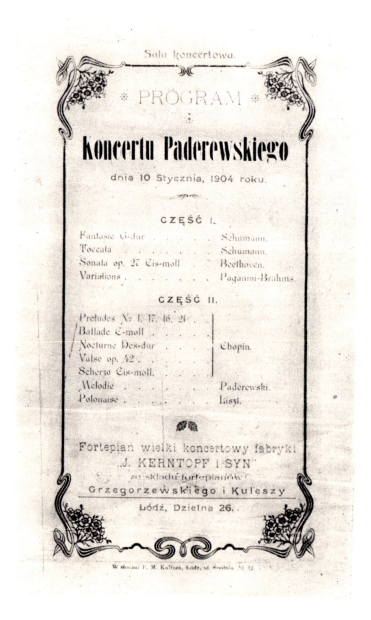

On his way to St. Petersburg in 1904, Paderewski gave a few charity concerts in Łódź and Cracow. After the outbreak of the Russo-Japanese War, he left Russia.

Виленскій Городской Залъ

2 Января 1904 года.

КОНЦЕРТЪ

знаменитаго піаниста

И. ПАДЕРЕВСКАГО.

Программа:

Fantaisie C-dur	Schumann.
Toccata.	Schumann.
Sonate op. 27 Cis-moll.	Beethoven.
Variations	Paganini-Brahms.
Ballade G-moll.	
Nocturne Des-dur.	
Valse op. 42.	Chopin
Scherzo Cis-moll.	
Mélodie.	Paderewski.
Polonaise.	Liszt.

Концертный рояль фабрики И. Керптопфъ и Сынъ въ ВАРШАВѢ

НАЧАЛО ВЪ 8 ЧАСОВЪ ВЕЧЕРА.

ПРОГРАММА.

Въ Залѣ Дворянскаго Собранія

Воскресенье, 4-го Января 1904 года

КОНЦЕРТЪ

извѣстнаго піаниста

И. Падеревскаго.

BACH LISZT
MENDELSSOHN
BEETHOVEN
SCHUMANN

CHOPIN

PADEREWSKI
LISZT

начало 8 час вечера.

ГОРОДЪ МИНСКЪ

ВЪ СУББОТУ 3 Января 1904 года

ВЪ ГОРОДСКОМЪ ТЕАТРѢ

состоятся

КОНЦЕРТЪ

знаменитаго піаниста

И. ПАДЕРЕВСКАГО

Программа:

Отдѣленіе 1-е.

Prelude et Fugue A-moll	Bach-Liszt
Sonate op. 53	Beethoven
2 Lieder ohne Worte	Mendelssohn
Etudes Symphoniques	Schumann

Отдѣленіе 2-е.

Ballade F-moll	
Etude op. 25 № 6, 7, 8	Chopin
Nocturne g-dur	
Polonaise As-dur	
Nocturne	Paderewski
Intermezzo polacco	
Rapsodie	Liszt

Начало ровно въ 8 часовъ вечера.

Концертный рояль фабрики Керптопфъ Варшавѣ

Въ залѣ Ремесленнаго Общества

Въ Вторникъ, 6-го Января 1904 года

въ 8 часовъ вечера

Единственный концертъ

Падеревскаго.

ПРОГРАММА

I. Шуманъ. Фантазія C-dur.
Токката.
II. Бетховенъ. Соната, op. 27 Cis-moll.
III. Брамсъ. Варіаціи за тему Паганини.

IV. Шопенъ. Баллада As-dur.
Ноктюрнъ H-dur.
Вальсъ op. 42.
Скерцо Cis-moll.
V. Падеревскій. Мелодія.
VI. Листъ. Полонезъ.

рояль Стейнвей и Сыновья, Нью-Іоркъ-Гамбургъ изъ главнаго депо П. Нейдмера.

Во время концерта входъ воспрещается.

Im Saale des Gewerbevereins

Dienstag, den 6. Januar 1904.

Abends 8 Uhr

Einmaliges Concert

Paderewski.

PROGRAMM.

I. Schumann. Fantaisie C-dur.
Toccata.
II. Beethoven. Sonate op. 27 Cis-moll.
III. Brahms. Variationen über ein Thema von Paganini.

IV. Chopin. Ballade As-dur.
Nocturne H-dur.
Valse op. 42.
Scherzo Cis-moll.
V. Paderewski. Mélodie.
VI. Liszt. Polonaise.

Concertflügel: Steinway & Sons. New-York-Hamburg. aus dem Dépôt P. Neidner.

Während der Vorträge bleiben die Saal- und Balconthüren geschlossen.

Buchdruckerei L. Blankenstein, Riga.

ЗАЛЪ „УНІОНЪ".

Въ Понедѣльникъ 2-го Февраля 1904 г.

КОНЦЕРТЪ

піаниста

И. ПАДЕРЕВСКАГО

ПРОГРАММА

Отдѣленіе 1-е

1) Fantaisie
2) Toccata
3) Sonate op. 27 Cis-moll
4) Variations

Отдѣленіе 2-е

5) a) Ballade As-dur
b) Nocturn H-dur
c) Valse Op. 42
d) Scherzo Cis-moll
6) Mélodie
7) Polonaise

Chopin

Paderewski
Liszt

Рояль фабрики Стейнвей и Сынъ изъ Депо Г. Э. Вицмана.

Начало въ 8½ часовъ вечера.

Билеты продаются въ нотномъ и книжномъ магазинѣ Э. Островскаго. Дерибасовская 26, противъ Пассажа.

Melbourne

He gave concerts in England and Germany and then embarked on a long tour of Australia and New Zealand. His failing health forced him to take a brief rest at the Rotorua Hot Spring Baths, known for their therapeutic qualities. The treatment was very helpful and he resumed the tour, which took him through many towns. His farewell concert in Melbourne was attended by seven thousand enthusiastic Australians.

After April, 1905, I did not play any more that year. I was not well. A complication of things, too subtle to disentangle now and of no interest really to our story, brought this about ...

Now, I must repeat again that I was not at all well in 1905 ... but nevertheless, in 1906, I made a tour in Spain. I played also in the South of France and Portugal, too. But that playing was not pleasant to me because something was happening to my nerves that made me completely hate the piano.[42]

The doctors recommended a total change in lifestyle. Accordingly, Paderewski bought a farm in Switzerland. This investment depleted his finances so badly that he was forced to return to the concert stage — giving two extensive tours in America, not to mention concerts in Europe. During Paderewski's second sojourn in America, his *Symphony* was first presented in Boston, December 1908, and later performed in Washington, Philadelphia, and Baltimore.

Again I tried in 1909 to play. I went to Monte Carlo and Nice, and then, just to find out whether I could play or not, I went on to Bordighera. But it was impossible.[43]

He commemorated the five hundredth anniversary of the Battle of Grunwald by donating to the Polish nation a gift of a monument created by the sculptor, Antoni Wiwulski.

...moc zwątpienia, w której i myśl się mroczy
chęć do czynu zamiera. Tylko w tej muzyc
kliwej a burzliwej, cichej a namiętnej, rzewne
mocnej i groźnej, w tej muzyce, co się rad
vymyka od dyscypliny metrycznej, co się uchyl,
d karności rytmu, co nie znosi metronomu, ja
nienawidzonego rządu, w tej muzyce słyszy się
zuje, poznaje, że naród nasz, ziemia nasza, ż
ała Polska żyje, czuje, działa: „in tempo ru
ato". Dlaczegoż w Szopenie właśnie ozwał
ię tak silnie dusza narodu, dlaczego z jego serc
łos rasy naszej, jak zdrój kryształowy z głębi
iemi niezbadanych, wytrysnął potężny, ożywczy
rzeczysty? Spytajmy o to Tego, który „łon
ajemnic odmyka"... On nam nie wszystko jesz
ze powiedział i bodaj że nigdy wszystkiego ni
owie... Zwyczajny „krwi polskiej" słuchacz
wielką sztuką muzyczną nieoswojony, arcydzie
Bacha, Mozarta, Beethovena słucha niechętnie, cza
em niecierpliwie. Kunsztowna wielogłosowoś
ogactwo przeróżnych dźwiękowych powikła
asne dla wyćwiczonego umysłu, niedostępne dl
ego ucha. Myśl jego się gubi w misternych fugac
waga się błąka i rozprasza wśród marmurowyc
ształtów pięknej, lecz germańskiej sonaty, w prze
dziwnych gmachach klasycznej symfonii zimn

The program of the Lvov Chopin Centennial Celebrations included the Polish première of Paderewski's *Symphony* and a production of *Manru*. Because his aversion to the piano still persisted, Paderewski did not give a concert, instead he delivered his now famous speech, published later in several languages.

And perhaps all unknowingly this proved to be my first real entrance into politics, the very beginning of a career that in the farthest stretches of my imagination I could not have foreseen.[44]

Arthur Nikisch

Henryk Sienkiewicz

Marcelina Sembrich-Kochańska

Zygmunt Stojowski

On the 31st of July, the day of my patron saint, St. Ignace, which has always been a day of festivity in my house, there was a very large gathering of people from various countries, and of many nationalities.

... [we] had no word to speak on that fateful day, August 1, 1914. War had been declared. The fate of Europe, perhaps the whole world, was in abeyance and all mankind with it. A new world, a new era was at hand, I felt sure, and I, too, must enter this new era, the era of an unexpected and fated career.[45]

The End of an Era

Alfred Northcliffe
Aristide Briand
Winston Churchill

"... the many cities in which he gave concerts offered
him opportunities of meeting those men whose conversation would turn not on music, but on politics:
Aristide Briand, Stephen Pichon, Lord Herbert As-
quith, Arthur Balfour, and Theodore Roosevelt. His
intimate friendships with many of the leading states-
men of Europe and America paved the way for future
political activity ...

Within a few years Paderewski came to be considered
one of the experts on matters connected with the
124 problems of Poland."[46]

ORCHESTRA HALL

SUNDAY, APRIL 22, 1917

3:00 P. M.

I. J. PADEREWSKI

PIANO RECITAL

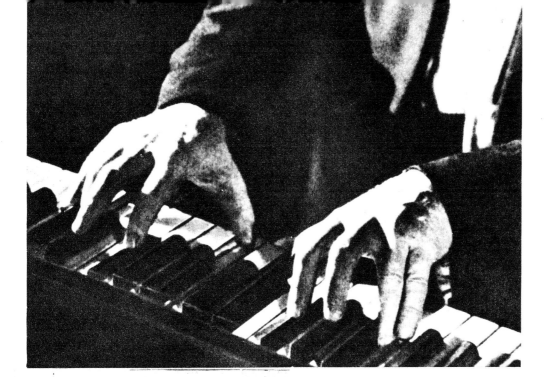

Polish Victims Relief Fund Benefit
Organized by the Biltmore Comstock Music School

**Grand Ballroom of the Hotel Biltmore
November 5th, 1915, 3 to 7 P. M.**
Admission $2.00

Lausanne, Vevey, the home of Henryk Sienkiewicz, and Morges became political centers for the Polish émigrés. One of their goals was to promote the not very popular Polish Cause both in French and British circles. Paderewski, together with Sienkiewicz, directed the activity of the Committee for Aid to Poles in the Homeland, established in Vevey. In February, 1915 he left for London via Paris where Paderewski's popularity and the support of his influential friends enabled him to establish the Polish Victims Relief Fund. Within a few months an impressive sum of 50,000 pounds sterling was collected.

The Committee carried on a very active campaign in the United States. President Wilson's wife wrote in her memoirs: "On Monday, November 6, 1919, I find recorded in my 'Line-a-day Book': 'At 2:30 a delegation headed by Mr. Paderewski arrived to ask W. Wilson to set aside a day to help the Poles ... Mr. P. ended with a beautiful tribute to my husband and expressed his utmost faith in him and his sincere desire to help these suffering people.'

I shall never forget Mr. Paderewski's face as he stood pleading the cause of his country. It was so fine, so tragic, so earnest. As I knelt there above them I felt I was witnessing through his eyes all the suffering and degradation of his countrymen. His hair was like a nimbus around his head. To have seen together these two men who were making the world better and happier is a memory I shall always cherish."[47]

Woodrow Wilson

"The task, first of officially establishing a Polish army for the Allies, and then of recruiting it, was a slow and difficult one … The actual organization of the force meant, of course, a good deal more than a matter of calling for volunteers. The machinery of recruiting had to be organized, the record of every volunteer justified, a training camp had to be established, provision made for transport and feeding … Paderewski's army … placed under the leadership of General Józef Haller, one of the most daring and picturesque of Poland's heroes, totalled nearly one hundred thousand men."[48]   **129**

With his wife

Paderewski set foot on Polish soil on Christmas Day, 1918. He accepted the office of Prime Minister and Minister of Foreign Affairs.

"I did not come for fame, honor or high office but to serve and not any specific political party. This is not the time for factions. There is only one party — that is Poland! I respect all of them but I do not belong and will not belong to any. In the face of the danger from the East, each son of this land has only the right to be a Pole. No party [by itself] will rebuild Poland. We will all rebuild it, and its foundations are the workers and the masses. Long live the Polish people and the Polish worker. Long live the [various] classes united and strong through mutual peace and love."[49]

Versailles

In April of 1919 Paderewski, the Polish delegate to the Versailles Peace Conference, arrived in Paris. On June 28th he signed the peace treaty with Germany.
"Honesty of means as well as honesty of purpose was evident in his conduct as a negotiator ... Confidence in his integrity was the natural consequence of acquaintance and intercourse with Mr. Paderewski, and it was the universality of this confidence that made him so influential with the delegates to the Peace Conference ..."[50]   **133**

Paderewski withdrew from all his political activities to find solace and rest in America. He returned to America in 1921, first to New York and then to his farm in California.

Helena Paderewska

A Great Man of His Time

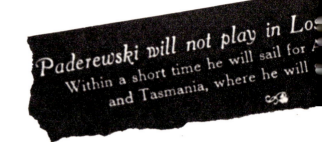

Paderewski will not play in Lo...
Within a short time he will sail for ...
and Tasmania, where he will

Concert
von
...gnaz Jan Paderewski.

Paderewski returned to his artistic life — he began traveling again, giving concerts in America, England, France, Belgium, and Switzerland. In 1927, he toured Australia again.

"All the intoxicating details of a virtuoso's life were back again: preparation of programs, traveling the new concert halls, the interviewers, and above all, the crowds. But his public had to be conquered anew. Paderewski's political career confused the issue in many people's minds."[51]

Angeles this season
tralia, New Zeal
e thirt

(by Arrangement with L. E. BEHYMER)

PADEREWSK

ary 18, 19

M. and M
P

ST. JAMES'S HALL

MONS

PADEREWSKI'S

FIRST

Pianoforte Recital,

FRIDAY AFTERNOON, MAY 9, 1890

J. PADEREWSK

PADEREWSKI

(Pianist) Professor des Warschauer Conservatorium

IGNACE PADEREWSKI
PIANO RECITAL

Under the Auspices of the American Legion,
For the Benefit of Disabled Polish Volunteers

I. J. Paderew

ONCERTO A TOTALE BENEFICIO
COMITATO PER LA PROTEZIONE
L' ASSISTENZA DEGLI ORFANI DI GUERR

CONCERTO DI

J. PADEREWSK

Per volontà del Maestro, l'incasso del concer
devoluto a totale beneficio del Comitato Nazionale
la Protezione ed Assistenza degli Orfani di Guerra

AUGUSTEO

STAGIONE 1924-25
XLI.

LUNEDI 4 MAGGIO 1925, ALLE ORE 17 PRECISE

CONCERTO STRAORDINARIO
GENTILMENTE OFFERTO DA

PADEREWSKI

A BENEFICIO DELL'OPERA NAZIONALE
PER GLI ORFANI DI GUERRA

E DEDICATO A

FEDERICO CHOPIN

E vietato entrare nella Sala o uscirne durante l'esecuzione dei pezzi.
NON SI CONCEDONO BIS

CONCERTO

I. J. PADEREWSKI

Organizzato dalla Società degli " Amici della Musica "
a totale beneficio del Comitato Nazionale per la
Protezione e l'Assistenza degli Orfani di Guerra.

Revenue from a number of concerts and even entire tours were donated for charities. In America, Paderewski gave benefit concerts for American and Polish war invalids, in Switzerland for the construction of a concert hall, in Lausanne for the rebuilding of a cathedral and the unemployed workers, in Italy for wartime orphans, in France for the building of dormitories for music students...

RÉCITAL DE GALA

donné par

PADEREWSKI

le plus grand Maitre du Clavier

au profit de

Association d'Aides aux Veuves de militaires de la Grande Guerre
(Œuvre reconnue d'utine publique, par decret du 29 février 1916)

Président : M. le Maréchal Foch.

Les places seront en vente à partir du Lundi 28 Mai de 10 h. à
de 2 h. à 5 heures à l'Ecole Normale de Musique, 64, rue Jouffroy

En venant elles-mêmes retirer leurs billets, les personnes pourront
le LIVRE D'OR qui sera offert à M. Paderewski en souvenir de cette s
dont le produit est destiné par le grand et généreux Artiste à la fonda
de bourses d'études pour élèves musiciens français.

au profit de la construction

d'une salle de concerts à Lausanne

donné par

I.-J. PADEREWSKI

With Queen Elizabeth of Belgium

Many universities conferred honorary degrees upon him. The first one was granted by the University of Lvov (1912) and was followed by Yale University (1917), the Jagiellonian University in Cracow (1919), Oxford University (1920), Columbia University (1922), University of Southern California (1923), University of Poznań (1924), University of Glasgow (1925), and Cambridge University (1926).

In the year 1924 he took part in the ceremonious transfer from Vevey to Poland the remains of his cherished friend, Henryk Sienkiewicz, who died in 1916.

" 'Are there any particular writers whom you consider greater than all others, and who are they?'

'Shakespeare, Molière and Gogol. Of all the Russian writers Gogol is for me the greatest. His *Dead Souls* and his *Revisor* are masterpieces conceived by one of the great literary geniuses of the world.'

'What about contemporary literature? Do you admire Bernard Shaw as much as most Poles do?'

'I like him and I enjoy his plays, which never fail to make me laugh; but I value him little. He is an excellent entertainer, brilliant and amusing, but not deep. There is nothing really creative in Shaw, and there is too much cynicism. I mistrust cynicism, and I value paradox only up to a point. It must remain an ornament and shouldn't become the very thing. I much prefer Galsworthy; I even prefer Wells.'

'What do you think of Aldous Huxley?'

'I don't know him; neither do I know the other young writers in England. I don't seem to find time for them. There is such a lot to read and to learn in life; there are innumerable scientific books that I am trying to get through and that somehow or other I missed in my earlier days. One must not forget that there are also endless novels that one ought to read again, Balzac for instance. In my opinion he is one of the most important novelists of all times.' "[52]

145

Francis Poulenc

José Iturbi

Vladimir Horowitz

"...By the time the post-war generation of pianists appeared, Paderewski's musical ideas were definitely set ... He could hardly be expected to enter whole-heartedly into the spirit of the era they represented. An almost boundless gulf separated them from each other; it was as though Paderewski's artistic achievement and that of Iturbi, Horowitz, Poulenc, Levitsky, Gieseking and Fischer were of different worlds."[53]   **147**

Richard Strauss

"... I decided to approach a matter which we had not yet discussed and which, although I knew him to be reluctant to talk about, I considered important enough to be mentioned: namely his own attitude towards comtemporary music and musicians. I began rather carefully:

'Do you consider that the Germans are still leading in the world of music?'

'No, certainly not. For me Richard Strauss is the last great German composer ... Otherwise, the creative musical genius seems to have shifted to France.'

'What about Pfitzner, about Schönberg, Webern, Hindemith, Alban Berg, Weill?'

'Don't ask me about them. Most of them belong to another generation that I don't understand, and there is little in common between them and myself.'

'Are there any great Polish composers living at present?'

'Szymanowski is undoubtedly a man of great talent. Some of his songs are quite lovely, and they can well be compared with the songs of any composer you may care to mention. His instrumental, and more particularly his piano compositions, however, do not mean a great deal to me; I cannot find contact with them, and I must confess that, although I tried to play one or two of them, I simply could not get into their spirit, and I was unable to find an interpretation for them ... His more recent compositions are too cold for me, too 'cérébrale'."[54]

Arnold Schönberg

Anton Webern

From left: Stanisław Szpinalski, Zygmunt Dygat, Ignacy Paderewski, Albert Tadlewski, Stanisław Nawrocki, Henryk Sztompka

Witold Małcużyński

Paderewski devoted a great deal of time to the teaching of music. Young pianists and composers would come to stay for the summer months at Riond-Bosson. Paderewski made sure that his pupils and their families were completely free of financial concerns. A group of young Polish pianists and composers, who were studying in Paris, were invited in the summer of 1929. Paderewski set up a schedule for them where they would gather together once a week to present the results of their work and listen to the master's instructions. The group included a number of the future talented composers and pianists: Zygmunt Dygat, Michał Kondracki, Feliks Łabuński, Stanisław Nawrocki, Piotr Perkowski, Stanisław Szpinalski, Henryk Sztompka, Albert Tadlewski. Two of them, Sztompka and Szpinalski, began their careers as virtuoso pianists. In the summer of 1937, Witold Małcużyński benefitted from Paderewski's guidance. **151**

ALHAMBRA PALACE HOTEL
NICE·CIMIEZ
OUVERT TOUTE L'ANNÉE
·
TÉLEPH. 26·29
73·42
···

7. 2. 1930.

Moja droga Siostrunia,

Z rozmowy telefonicznej, przeprowadzonej
przez Helenkę z jakimś uszczegawanym
przez Ciebie anonymem, dowiedziałaś się
już, jeśmy tu dojechali szczęśliwie. Nie
zawiastem sam o tem telegraficznie, za co
najpokornić przepraszam, ale przyznaję
otwarcie, że w smutku i przygnębieniu
jakoś mi to na myśl nie przyszło.

Biedną naszą Helenkę zastałem
w stanie gorszym, niż przed jej wyjazdem
z Riond. Schudła bardzo. Jakiś ciągły
niepokój ją dręczy. Ciągle pracę i mówi
ciągle, niestety, same niezgaduniat rzeczy.

A sudden illness made impossible Paderewski's planned winter tour in 1929. His wife's health also was deteriorating.

152

With Antonina Paderewska-Wilkońska

"... In October Paderewski developed a swelling in both legs and a particularly bad form of phlebitis, which forced him to remain in the nursing home for months. He left it just in time to spend Christmas at Riond-Bosson, but he was still far from well. After a short stay at home he decided to go to Nice; but even there he did not recover and there were days when the pain of the swelling in his legs prevented him from walking. As playing the piano was still a financial necessity to Paderewski, and as for many months he had not been able to touch that instrument, he decided to go to Paris without further delay, though it was doubtful whether he would be restored to health in time to start another tour the same year. But the old stubborn pride prevented him from giving way or betraying his real state of health.

This characteristic was demonstrated very strikingly on the day Paderewski was to leave for Paris. He wished to leave Nice quietly and did not disclose the date or hour of his departure to any one ... When he appeared on the platform accompanied by two or three friends there was quite a crowd of admirers waiting to see him ... Each step gave him pain. As long as he walked on level ground he could contrive to walk without limping or suffering unduly; but to climb the few steep steps into the railway carriage without showing signs of pain would be quite impossible. The bell rang. The sweat on Paderewski's forehead was the only thing that betrayed the nervous strain through which he was passing. No, he could not possibly climb these steps; rather would he let the train go without him. On the second when the train actually began to move, he jumped up the three steps with all the vigor of a young man. But his friends on the platform could not see that inside the carriage Marcel had just picked up his master on the verge of collapse, his face distorted with pain and almost unrecognizable."[55]

After a long period of recuperation, Paderewski resumed his concert tours in Europe and the United States.

He returned to Riond-Bosson in May 1931 for a prolonged rest. His general exhaustion caused by intense artistic activity, and deteriorating health of his wife, prevented him from resuming his concert tours.

Mr. I. J. Paderewski
begs to offer the expression of his
deep abiding gratitude for your
sympathy.

A grave blow for Paderewski in 1934 — his wife died on January 16. Her death undermined the artist's strength and his apparently indestructible energy.

158

"From the moment Mme. Helena fell in love with Paderewski, it was not only her future husband whom she worshipped in him, but also the outstanding artist. Although intellectually he was her superior, she was able to substitute an accurate instinct for what she lacked in culture and musical education ... Things she did not know she seemed to acquire by a process of emotional assimilation. He represented to her everything that an heroic genius might mean to one who was not only an adoring wife but also a sensitive woman ... It was perhaps a strange mixture — romantic adoration and a strong instinct in an otherwise matter-of-fact woman — but they became the guiding principles of her married life with Ignace ... She helped him most efficiently in all the thousand little details of a life preoccupied with art; she protected him from people; she saw to it that he always had the right conditions for work, for leisure and enjoyment; she stimulated him to ceaseless work; she prevented him from spending too much money and restrained people from taking advantage of his generosity ...

Even more important than her assistance in the petty difficulties of an artist's existence was the less tangible psychological help which she was able to afford. Paderewski was very highly strung, and his work and his eminent position increased that natural tendency. Behind his mental energy there was his artistic disposition, and his romantic point of view, neither of which could thrive in a banal domesticity. The counterbalance of serious realism was provided by many long hours of hard work, which were the sobering element of his day. Mme. Helena must have known instinctively that it would be wrong to put their personal relations on a basis of prosaic sobriety."[56]

In 1935 Paderewski gave a few concerts in Switzerland but the tour had to be cancelled because of his exhaustion and poor health. He rested for a full year under close medical supervision.

In the spring of 1936 his health improved. He was able to fulfill an earlier commitment to make a motion picture, *Moonlight Sonata*, produced by British filmmakers, which today constitutes a unique document.

"The cinema had become one of Paderewski's favorite pastimes. When he had old friends to dine with him in London, Paris, or New York and it was not a ceremonial occasion, he liked asking them to an early meal and then going on to a cinema. There was no sophistication nor aestheticism about his cinematographic taste, and while the picture flickered across the screen, he liked to believe that the events of the film were real. There seems to be a decided analogy between his attitude to a cinema and to that of his more serious preoccupations. All through his life Paderewski's sense of reality was based on a peculiar kind of faith: it was faith in all the illusions of life which furnished it with an aspect of greater beauty. He had achieved his political successes through his firm belief in ideals that for other politicians had been only illusions. In a way, he was also trying to create illusions on the piano."[57]

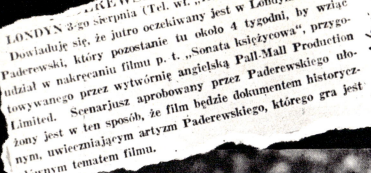

...REWSKI W LONDYNIE.

LONDYN 3-go sierpnia (Tel. wł. „Kurjera Warszawskiego)

Dowiaduję się, że jutro oczekiwany jest w Londynie Ignacy Paderewski, który pozostanie tu około 4 tygodni, by wziąć udział w nakręcaniu filmu p. t. „Sonata księżycowa", przygotowywanego przez wytwórnię angielską Pall-Mall Production Limited. Scenarjusz aprobowany przez Paderewskiego ułożony jest w ten sposób, że film będzie dokumentem historycznym, uwieczniającym artyzm Paderewskiego, którego gra jest głównym tematem filmu.

Za kilka tygodni będzie pokazywany w Chicago film, wykończony ostatnio w Londynie pod tytułem "The Moonlight Sonata", w ktcrej gra na fortepianie Ignacy Jan Paderewski, uwieczniony na zawsze w filmie.

With Józef Turczyński

The pianist, Józef Turczyński, delegated by the Frederic Chopin Institute in Warsaw, came to Riond-Bosson in 1937 with a proposal to Paderewski — that he become editor of a new edition of Chopin's complete works. The offer was accepted. The first volumes (*Preludes, Ballades*) edited by Paderewski with the cooperation of Turczyński and Ludwik Bronarski, were ready for print early in 1939.

Nowe Wydanie Dzieł Szopena

Warszawa, 25. września. (PAT.) — Instytut im. Fryderyka Szopena w Warszawie pracuje nad wydaniem kompletnej edycji dzieł Szopena, przyczym wydawcy opierają się na oryginalnych rękopisach przejrzanych i zatwierdzonych przez Paderewskiego. Materiał do druku przygotowuje specjalna komisja w skład której wchodzą prof. Józef Turczyński, dr. B. Keuprulian-Wójcik i dr. L. Bronarski. Dwa wydawnictwa gotowe już są do druku:

a) oryginały Szopena z autentycznym tekstem z rękopisów lub z pierwszego wydania i

b) specjalne wydanie dla szkół.

Instytut im. Fryderyka Szopena, który przedsięwział tę pracę jest organizacją społeczną, na której czele stoi August Zaleski, były minister spraw zagranicznych.

Adres Instytutu jest: Plac Dąbrowskiego 2. Warszawa.

The world-shattering events during September, 1939 brought insufferable pain and shock to Paderewski. He left for the United States in the fall of 1940 and, upon arriving in New York, he was ceremoniously greeted by the American populace. That night, a New York radiostation showed its appreciation by airing a full program devoted to his career. Pianists throughout America donated their concert proceeds to aid Poland. Paderewski's goal remained constant — to help his beloved and beleagured Poland. He resumed old friendships and made new ones, attended fund-raising rallies, and did everything in his power to help his country in time of her greatest need.

166

To celebrate the fiftieth anniversary of his first concert in America, a Paderewski Week was organized, at which a cable from President Roosevelt opened the ceremonies.

"...you have merited abundantly the accolade of 'Modern Immortal' which an appreciative public has bestowed on you in recognition of gifts and talents which you have shared so generously... To a superb artist, to a patriot and lover of freedom in whose cause you have worked with valor and gallantry, I offer heartfelt felicitations."[58] **169**

In June, 1941, in spite of warnings from those close to him, Paderewski participated in a rally for Veterans of the Polish Army. He delivered his last speech there. He came down with pneumonia and within three days, on June 29, 1941, Ignacy Jan Paderewski was dead. His body was buried in a crypt at Arlington National Cemetery, the resting place of many heroes who fought for freedom and justice in the United States.

Footnotes

[1] Ignace Jan Paderewski and Mary Lawton, *The Paderewski Memoirs*, New York, 1938, pp. 1–4.

[2] *Ibid.*, pp. 9–20.

[3] *Ibid.*, pp. 17–20.

[4] *Ibid.*, pp. 15–27.

[5] *Ibid.*, pp. 36–37.

[6] *Ibid.*, pp. 45–46.

[7] *Ibid.*, p. 56.

[8] *Ibid.*, pp. 61–63.

[9] *Ibid.*, p. 65.

[10] *Ibid.*, p. 60.

[11] *Ibid.*, pp. 64, 100.

[12] *Ibid.*, p. 63.

[13] *Ibid.*, p. 67.

[14] *Ibid.*, p. 81.

[15] *Ibid.*, p. 15.

[16] *Memories and Impressions of Helena Modjeska : An Autobiography,* New York, 1910, pp. 205, 468.

[17] *Paderewski Memoirs, op. cit.,* pp. 93, 94.

[18] Rom Landau, *Ignace Paderewski : Musician and Statesman,* New York, 1934, pp. 14–16.

[19] *Paderewski Memoirs, op. cit.,* p. 91.

[20] *Ibid.*, pp. 91–92, 97.

[21] *Ibid.*, pp. 101–102.

[22] *Ibid.*, pp. 108–109, 111, 112, 114.

[23] *Ibid.*, pp. 115–16.

[24] Landau, *op. cit.,* p. 22.

[25] *Paderewski Memoirs, op. cit.,* pp. 134, 135, 136.

[26] *Ibid.*, p. 119.

[27] *Ibid.*, pp. 122, 123.

[28] *Ibid.*, p. 129.

[29] *Ibid.*, p. 162.

[30] Ignacy Jan Paderewski and Mary Lawton, *The Paderewski Memoirs*, London: Collins, 1939, pp. 15–16.

[31] *Paderewski Memoirs, op. cit.,* pp. 174, 175, 183–84.

[32] Landau, *op. cit.,* p. 35.

[33] *Paderewski Memoirs, op. cit.,* pp. 190, 219–20.

[34] Landau, *op. cit.,* pp. 72, 73.

[35] *Paderewski Memoirs, op. cit.,* pp. 204–5.

[36] *Ibid.*, p. 300.

[37] *Ibid.*, pp. 268, 281, 307.

[38] 'Goniec Wieczorny' (Evening Courier), Warsaw, 1904, no. 18.

[39] *Paderewski Memoirs, op. cit.,* pp. 315, 316.

[40] Landau, *op. cit.* p. 62.

[41] *Paderewski Memoirs, op. cit.,* pp. 326–27.

[42] *Ibid.*, pp. 364, 366.

[43] *Ibid.*, p. 372.

[44] *Ibid.*, pp. 375–76.

[45] *Ibid.*, pp. 393, 397.

[46] Landau, *op. cit.*, p. 104.

[47] Edith Bollin Wilson, *My Memoir*, Indianapolis, 1939, p. 113.

[48] Charles Phillips, *Paderewski, The Story of a Modern Immortal*, New York, 1933, pp. 352–53.

[49] Speech by Paderewski upon his arrival in Poland, Jan. 2, 1919. 'Gazeta Warszawska' (Warsaw Daily), January 7, 1919, p. 3.

[50] In the opinion of Robert Lansing, then American Undersecretary of State, cf. Robert Lansing, *The Big Four and Others of the Peace Conference*, Boston, 1921, p. 212.

[51] Landau, *op. cit.*, pp. 157–58.

[52] *Ibid.*, p. 273.

[53] *Ibid.*, p. 227.

[54] *Ibid.*, pp. 282, 285.

[55] *Ibid.*, pp. 221–22.

[56] *Ibid.*, pp. 87–89.

[57] *Ibid.*, p. 245.

[58] Franklin D. Roosevelt to Ignacy Jan Paderewski, February, 4, 1941, Franklin D. Roosevelt MSS, *Franklin D. Roosevelt Library*, Hyde Park, New York.

List of Compositions
(compiled by Małgorzata Perkowska)

Op. 1. ca 1886. *Zwei Klavierstücke*: a. *Prélude à capriccio*, b. *Minuetto* in g-minor. Bote & Bock, Berlin ca 1886.

Op. 2. ca 1881. *Trois morceaux* for piano: *Gavotte* in e-minor, *Mélodie* in C-major, *Valse mélancolique* in A-major (dedicated to Theresa Wlasoff). Kruziński & Lewi, Warsaw 1881.

Op. 4. 1883. *Élégie* for piano. Bote & Bock, Berlin 1883.

Op. 5. ca 1883. *Danses polonaises* for piano: *Krakowiak* in E-major, *Mazurek* in e-minor, *Krakowiak* in B-flat major (dedicated to Natalia Janotha). Bote & Bock, Berlin 1883; version for 4 hands (with Op. 9) ca 1892.

Op. 6. ca 1884. *Introduction et Toccata* for piano. Bote & Bock, Berlin 1884.

Op. 7. ca 1885. *Vier Lieder (Four Songs)* to poems by Adam Asnyk, for voice and piano: 1. *Gdy ostatnia róża zwiędła (The Day of Roses)*, 2. *Siwy koniu (To My Faithful Steed)*, 3. *Szumi w gaju brzezina (The Birch Tree and the Maiden)*, 4. *Chłopca mego mi zabrali (My Love is Sent Away)*. Bote & Bock, Berlin ca 1886.

Op. 8. ca 1883. *Chants du voyageur*, five pieces for piano: 1. *Allegro agitato*, 2. *Andantino*, 3. *Andantino grazioso (Melody* in B-major*)* also for violin and cello with piano and for orchestra, 4. *Andantino mistico*, 5. *Allegro giocoso* (dedicated to Helena Górska). Bote & Bock, Berlin 1883.

Op. 9. ca 1883. *Danses polonaises* for piano. Book I: 1. *Krakowiak* in F-major, 2. *Mazurek* in a-minor and 3. A-major, Book II: 4. *Mazurek* in B-flat major, 5. *Krakowiak* in A-major, 6. *Polonaise* in B-major. Bote & Bock, Berlin 1884–85; version for 4 hands (with Op. 5) ca 1892.

Op. 10. ca 1884. *Album de mai, scènes romantiques*, for piano: 1. *Au soir*, 2. *Chant d'amour*, 3. *Scherzino*, 4. *Barcarolle*, 5. *Caprice (Valse)* (dedicated to Anette Essipoff-Leschetizky). Bote & Bock, Berlin 1884.

Op. 11. ca 1883. *Variations et Fugue sur un thème original* in a-minor, for piano. Bote & Bock, Berlin ca 1885.

Op. 12. ca 1883. *Tatra Album, Tänze und Lieder des polnischen Volkes aus Zakopane* (dedicated to Tytus Chałubiński). Ries & Erler, Berlin 1883–84; for 4 hands 1884.

Op. 13. 1882. *Sonate pour violon et piano* in a-minor (dedicated to Pablo Sarasate). Bote & Bock, Berlin 1885.

Op. 14. ca 1887. *Humoresques de concert* for piano. Book I *(à l'antique)*: 1. *Menuet célèbre*, 2. *Sarabande*, 3. *Caprice (genre Scarlatti)*; Book II *(à la moderne)*: 4. *Burlesque*, 5. *Intermezzo polacco*, 6. *Cracovienne fantastique*. Bote & Bock, Berlin 1887, 1888.

Op. 15. ca 1888. *Dans le désert, tableau musical en forme d'une toccata*, for piano (dedicated to Anette Essipoff-Leschetizky). Bote & Bock, Berlin ca 1888.

Op. 16. ca 1888. *Miscellanea*, series of piano pieces: 1. *Légende No. 1* in A-flat major, 2. *Mélodie* in G-flat major, 3. *Thème varié* in A-major, 4. *Nocturne* in B-flat major, 5. *Légende No. 2* in A-major, 6. *Un moment musical*, 7. *Menuet* in A-major. Bote & Bock, Berlin ca 1888-94.

No. 6: *Un moment musical* published in 'Echo Muzyczne i Teatralne' (Musical and Theatrical Echo), 1892, No. 435, Warsaw.

Op. 17. 1888. *Concerto* in a-minor for piano and orchestra (dedicated to Theodor Leschetizky). Bote & Bock, Berlin 1890.

Op. 18. 1893. *Sześć pieśni (Six Songs)* to words by Adam Mickiewicz, for voice and piano: 1. *Polały się łzy (Mine Eyes Have Known Tears)*, 2. *Piosnka dudarza (The Piper's Song)*, 3. *Moja pieszczotka (My Own Sweet Maiden)*, 4. *Nad wodą wielką i czystą (By Mighty Waters)*, 5. *Tylem wytrwał (Pain Have I Endured)*, 6. *Gdybym się zmienił (Might I But Change Me)* (dedicated to Władysław Mickiewicz). Bote & Bock, Berlin 1893.

Op. 19. 1893. *Polish Fantasy on Original Themes* for piano and orchestra (dedicated to Princess R. Bassaraba de Brancovan). Bote & Bock, Berlin 1893; G. Schirmer, New York.

Op. 20. 1892–1901. *Manru*, lyrisches Drama in drei Aufzügen. Libretto in German by Alfred Nossig, based on the novel *Chata za wsią (A Cottage Outside the Village)* by Józef Ignacy Kraszewski. Bote & Bock, Berlin 1901; piano score with English and German texts, G. Schirmer, New York. (First performance Dresden, May 29, 1901.).

Op. 21. ca 1903. *Sonata* in e-flat minor for piano. Bote & Bock, Berlin 1903.

Op. 22. ca 1903. *Douze mélodies* sur des poésies de Catulle Mendès. 12 Songs for voice and piano: 1. *Dans la forêt*, 2. *Ton coeur est d'or pur*, 3. *Le ciel est très bas*, 4. *Naguère*, 5. *Le jeune Pâtre*, 6. *Elle marche d'un pas distrait*, 7. *La jeune nonne*, 8. *Viduité*, 9. *Lune froide*, 10. *Querelleuse*, 11. *L'amour fatal*, 12. *L'ennemie*. Heugel, Paris 1903.

Op. 23. ca 1903. *Variations et fugue sur un thème original* in e-flat minor, for piano. Bote & Bock, Berlin 1903.

Op. 24. 1903–9. *Symphony* in b-minor 'Polonia'. Heugel, Paris 1911. (First perf. February 12, 1909).

Additional Compositions

Valse mignonne for piano, ca 1876 (dedicated to Gustaw Roguski).

Suite in E-flat major, for piano, ca 1879.

Impromptu for piano, ca 1879. Published in 'Echo Muzyczne i Teatralne' (Musical and Theatrical Echo), 1879, No. 11, Warsaw.

Dwa kanony (Two Canons) for piano. 'Echo Muzyczne i Teatralne', 1882, No. 19, Warsaw.

Krakowiak (Fantasy) for piano, 1884. 'Echo Muzyczne i Teatralne', 1887, No. 117, Warsaw (see also Op. 14, No. 6).

Powódź (The Flood). Leaflet *Na powodzian* issued in Warsaw for the benefit of the Polish flood victims, 1884.

2 Intermezzi: in g-minor and C-major, for piano, ca 1885. 'Echo Muzyczne i Teatralne', 1885, No. 77 (I), and No. 89 (II), Warsaw.

Canzone, chant sans paroles for piano, ca 1904. Bote & Bock, Berlin ca 1904.

Hej, Orle biały (Hey, White Eagle), hymn for male chorus and piano or wind orchestra. Words by composer, 1917. New York 1918 (?); K. T. Barwicki, Poznań 1926.

Sketches of Studies for piano.

List of Recordings

(compiled by Kornel Michałowski)

Four Songs to poems by Adam Asnyk, Op. 7
No. 1: Gdy ostatnia róża zwiędła (The Day of Roses)
1. Muza 1681 (1951): Maria Drewniakówna — soprano, Jerzy Lefeld — piano.
2. Muza SXL-1174 (1975): Elżbieta Jaroszewicz — soprano, Wacław Gay — piano.

No. 3: Szumi w gaju brzezina (The Birch Tree and the Maiden)
1. Muza 1681 (1951): Maria Drewniakówna — soprano, Jerzy Lefeld — piano.

Chants du voyageur, Op. 8
1. Music Library Records (USA) 7017 (ca 1954): R. Corbett — piano.

No. 3: Melody in B-major
1. His Master's Voice DA 577 (1923) = DB 3709 (1938): I. J. Paderewski — piano.
2. Classic Editions (USA) CE 1024 (ca 1954): E. Burton — piano.
3. Muza L 0144 (1958) — EX 0114 (1962): Józef Śmidowicz — piano.
4. Muza XL 0097 (1960): Ryszard Bakst — piano.

— arranged for orchestra
1. Muza 1281 (1948): symphony orchestra, conducted by Feliks Rybicki.

Danses polonaises, Op. 9
No. 1: Krakowiak in F-major
1. Muza L 0144 (1958) = EX 0114 (1962): Józef Śmidowicz — piano.

No. 3: Mazurek in A-major
1. Muza XL 0097 (1960): Ryszard Bakst — piano.

No. 5: Krakowiak in A-major (arranged for violin and piano)
1. Columbia DM 1721 (1933): Wacław Niemczyk — violin, Ludwik Urstein — piano.

Album de mai, Op. 10
No. 1: Au soir
1. Polydor 90040 (before 1931): Raul Koczalski — piano.

No. 2: Chant d'amour
1. Muza XL 0097 (1960): Ryszard Bakst — piano.

Tatra Album, Op. 12
fragments: *Dance and Song of Mountaineers* (arranged for orchestra)
1. Muza 1551–1552 (1950): symphony orchestra, cond. by Feliks Rybicki.

Sonata for violin and piano, in a-minor, Op. 13
1. Muza XL 0505 (1969): Edward Statkiewicz — violin, Aleksander Utrecht — piano.
2. Desmar DSM-1004 (1975): Endre Granat — violin, Harold Gray — piano.

Humoresques de Concert, Op. 14
No. 1: Menuet célèbre in G-major
1. His Master's Voice DB 379 (1912) = DB 604 (1917) = Columbia (USA) ML 4294 (ca 1950) =
   = Eurodisc 27674 XDK (1976): I. J. Paderewski — piano.

2. Columbia L 1391 (before 1925): Józef Hofmann — piano.
3. His Master's Voice DB 1090 = RCA Victor 6690 (1926): I. J. Paderewski — piano.
4. RCA Victor 6731 (ca 1928) = Argo DA-42 = RCA Victor AVM 3–0294 = Klavier KS–123 (1973): Sergey Rachmaninoff — piano.
5. Columbia 9372 = 5079 M (ca 1928): William Murdoch — piano.
6. Pathé X 98145 (before 1935): N. Ansay — piano.
7. Syrena-Electro 7787 (before 1935): P. Yenovitch — piano.
8. His Master's Voice DB 3124 = RCA Victor 16250 (1937) = RCA Victor LCT 1000 (ca 1950) = = Muza XL 0157 (1963) = XL 0684 (1971): I. J. Paderewski — piano.
9. Columbia DX 779 = 68987 D = DOX 544 (1937): Ignacy Friedman — piano.
10. His Master's Voice DA 6014 (ca 1945): S. Gyr — piano.
11. His Master's Voice DB 6468 = RCA Victor 11–9514 (ca 1945): = His Master's Voice 7 RF 288 = RCA Victor ERA 53 (ca 1954): José Iturbi — piano.
12. Philips N 11236 G (ca 1951) = S 06016 R (ca 1954): Marinus Flipse — piano.
13. Brunswick LA 8634 = Decca DL 5486 (ca 1954): C. Brown — piano.
14. Royale (USA) 1550 (ca 1954): E. Silver — piano.
15. Muza L 0152 (1958): Stanisław Szpinalski — piano.
16. Muza XL 0097 (1960) = L 0446 (1965): Ryszard Bakst — piano.
17. Musical Heritage Society (USA) MHS-1139 (1971): Alfred Kann — piano.
18. Musical Heritage Society (USA) MHS–1730 (1973): Alicia de Larocha — piano.
19. Connoisseur Society (USA) CS–2059 = CSQ–2059 (1974): J. Estrin — piano.
20. Saga 5400 (ca 1975): Edward Moore — piano.
— arranged for piano and orchestra
1. Telefunken TW 30027 (ca 1954): Willy Stech — piano, Philharmonic Orchestra in Hamburg, cond. by Bruno Wal-Berg.
— arranged for 4 pianos
1. RCA Victor 12-0207 (ca 1945): First Pianoforte Quartet.
— arranged for violin and piano
1. His Master's Voice DA 267 = RCA Victor 718 (before 1925): Fritz Kreisler — violin, with piano accompaniment.
2. Columbia LF 82 = LW 14 (ca 1928): Miguel Candéla — violin, Maurice Fauré — piano.
3. RCA Victor 10-1035 (before 1950): Henryk Szeryng — violin, R. Locatelli — piano.
4. Decca LXT 5012 = London LL 1171 (ca 1954): Alfred Campoli — violin, Eric Gritton — piano.
— arranged for violoncello and piano
1. Columbia LX 158 (ca 1932) = Telefunken A 2158 (1937): Gasper Cassadó — cello, Michael Raucheisen — piano.
2. His Master's Voice K 6425 (before 1936): Marcelli-Herson — cello, with piano accompaniment.
3. Supraphon SUF 20065 = FLPM 448 (before 1962): Vladimir Orlov — cello, Alfred Holeček — piano.
— arranged for orchestra
1. Syrena-Electro 6485 (before 1935): orchestra, cond. by Aleksander Sielski.
2. Clangor M 1565 (ca 1935): music ensemble of Berlin Philharmonic, cond. by Theo Mackeben.
3. RCA Victor 21650 = 20169 (before 1936): RCA Victor Concert Orchestra.
4. Parlophone E 10600 = Decca 25769 (before 1936): Edith Lorand Orchestra.

5. His Master's Voice 3026 (before 1936): Mark Weber Orchestra.

6. Decca F 1619 (before 1936): Hastings Orchestra.
7. Decca Y 5626 = 2344 (before 1950): Oxford Ensemble.
8. RCA Victor 45-5026 = 45-5076 (before 1950): RCA Victor Orchestra, cond. by Connell.
9. RCA Victor 26613 (before 1950): RCA Victor Ensemble, cond. by Rizzi.
10. Columbia DOX 744 = 71306 D (before 1950): André Kostelanetz Orchestra.
11. Columbia 35728 (before 1950): Salon Orchestra, cond. by Palitz.
12. Muza 1281 (1948): symphony orchestra, cond. by Feliks Rybicki.
13. Columbia GL 510 (ca 1951): Columbia Orchestra.
14. Columbia CBS 71063: Philadelphia Symphony Orchestra, cond. by Eugene Ormandy.
15. Capitol SMK 73952: Capitol Symphony Orchestra, cond. by Carmen Dragon.
16. Fontana 6736003 = K 71 BC 801: Leipzig Radio Symphony Orchestra, cond. by Robert Hanell.
17. Polydor 249155 = 2630004: Promenadenorchester, cond. by Hans Carste.
18. Telefunken NT 462: Philharmonische Staatsorchester Hamburg, cond. by Bruno Wal-Berg.
19. Muza SXL 1037 (1975): Warsaw String Orchestra, cond. and arr. by Marek Sewen.

No 3: Caprice (genre Scarlatti) in G major
1. Columbia 4156 (ca 1928): Leslie England — piano.
2. Columbia 4829 = 01055 = 2122 M (ca 1929): Lev Pouishnov — piano.
3. International Piano Library IPL 5005-06 (1976): Fernando Valenti — piano.

No. 5: Intermezzo polacco
1. Muza L 0144 (1958): Józef Śmidowicz — piano.
2. Muza XL 0097 (1960): Ryszard Bakst — piano.

No. 6: Cracovienne fantastique
1. His Master's Voice DB 379 (1912) = DB 683 = RCA Victor (1917) = Eurodisc 27674 XDK (1976): I. J. Paderewski — piano.
2. His Master's Voice B 2510 (before 1935): U. Bourne — piano.
3. Brunswick B 1072 = A 8924 (before 1935): Ignacy Hilsberg — piano.
4. Odeon 125133 (before 1950): Witold Małcużyński — piano.
5. Columbia (Japan) J 5594 (before 1950): Leonid Kreutzer — piano.
6. Muza XL 0097 (1960): Ryszard Bakst — piano.
— arranged for orchestra
1. Syrena-Electro 6484 (before 1935): orchestra, cond. by Aleksander Sielski.
2. Muza 1552 (1950): symphony orchestra, cond. by Feliks Rybicki.

Miscellanea, Op. 16
No. 1: Légende No. 1 in A-flat major
1. His Master's Voice B 2510 (before 1935): U. Bourne — piano.
2. Muza XL 0097 (1960): Ryszard Bakst — piano.
3. International Piano Archives IPA 102 (1976): Arthur Loeser — piano.

No. 2: Mélodie in G-flat major
1. Muza XL 0097 (1960): Ryszard Bakst — piano.
— arranged for violin and piano by Fritz Kreisler
1. His Master's Voice DA 511 = RCA Victor 947 (before 1925): Fritz Kreisler — violin, with piano accompaniment.
2. Homochord 4-2273 (before 1935): George Eweler — violin, with piano accompaniment.   **179**

— arranged for orchestra
1. Muza 1280 (1948): symphony orchestra, cond. by Feliks Rybicki.

No. 3: Thème varié in A-major
1. Muza XL 0097 (1960): Ryszard Bakst — piano.
2. Klavier KS-501 (1972): Nicolaisen — piano.
3. Vanguard VRS 1119 (1964) = Pye/Vanguard VSD 71119 (1968, 1972): Earl Wild — piano.
— arranged for a string quartet
1. Columbia 68933 D = LOX 352 (before 1960): Stradivarius Quartet.

No. 4: Nocturne in B-flat major
1. His Master's Voice DB 380 = RCA Victor 6232 (1917): I. J. Paderewski — piano.
2. Muza 1334 (1949): Józef Śmidowicz — piano.
3. Classic Editions (USA) CE 1026 (ca 1954): E. Burton — piano.
4. Muza L 0144 (1958): Józef Śmidowicz — piano.
5. Muza XL 0097 (1960): Ryszard Bakst — piano.

Concerto in a-minor for piano and orchestra, Op. 17
1. His Master's Voice C 3155-3158 = RCA Victor 15713-15716 (ca 1940): Jesús María Sanromá — piano, Boston Promenade Orchestra, cond. by Arthur Fiedler.
2. Muza XL 0196 (1964): Barbara Hesse-Bukowska — piano, Great Symphony Orchestra of Polish Radio, cond. by Jan Krenz.
3. Turnabout STV 34387 (1970) = Vox TV — S 34387 (1972): Felicja Blumenthal — piano, the "Pro Musica" Symphony Orchestra in Vienna, cond. by Helmuth Froschauer.
4. Victor LSC-3190 (1971): Earl Wild — piano, London Symphony Orchestra, cond. by Arthur Fiedler.

Sześć pieśni (Six Songs) to words by Adam Mickiewicz, Op. 18
1. Musette (ca 1940–45): Alfred Orda — bass, with piano accompaniment.

No. 1: Polały się łzy (Mine Eyes Have Known Tears)
1. Muza 1239 (1948): Alina Bolechowska — soprano, Jerzy Lefeld — piano.

No. 2: Piosnka dudarza (The Piper's Song)
1. Orpheon 136 (1938): Aniela Szlemińska — soprano, Jerzy Lefeld — piano.
2. Muza L 0444 (1965): Kazimierz Pustelak — tenor, Jerzy Marchwiński — piano.
— arranged for voice and orchestra by Olgierd Straszyński
1. Muza 1238 (1948): Alina Bolechowska — soprano, symphony orchestra, cond. by Olgierd Straszyński.
— arranged for chorus by Stanisław Wiechowicz *(The Piper)*
1. Muza XL 0164 (1963): Boys' and Men's Choir of the Poznań State Philharmonic, cond. by Stefan Stuligrosz.
2. Muza XL 0506 (1969): Poznań Boys' Choir, cond. by Jerzy Kurczewski.

No. 4: Nad wodą wielką i czystą (By Mighty Waters)
1. Muza 1352 (1949): Maria Drewniakówna — soprano, Jerzy Lefeld — piano.

No. 5: Tylem wytrwał (Pain Have I Endured)
1. Muza 1604 (1950): Józef Korolkiewicz — baritone, Jerzy Lefeld — piano.

No. 6: Gdybym się zmienił (Might I But Change Me)
1. Muza 1239 (1948): Alina Bolechowska — soprano, Jerzy Lefeld — piano.

Polish Fantasy on Original Themes, Op. 19
1. Decca LXT 2975 = London LL 1104 (ca 1954): Felicja Blumenthal — piano, London Symphony Orchestra, cond. by Anatole Fistoulari.
2. Muza XL 0114 (1961): Regina Smendzianka — piano, National Philharmonic Orchestra, cond. by Stanisław Wisłocki.
3. Turnabout STV 34345 (1970) = Everest 3376 (1976): Felicja Blumenthal — piano, Innsbruck Symphony Orchestra, cond. by Robert Wagner.
4. Victor LSC-3190 (1971): Earl Wild — piano, London Symphony Orchestra, cond. by Arthur Fiedler

— fragments
1. Columbia DMX 163 (ca 1925): Zbigniew Drzewiecki — piano, Warsaw Philharmonic Orchestra, cond. by Grzegorz Fitelberg.

Manru, Opera in 3 acts, Op. 20
Manru's aria from Act II '*Jako gdy wśród skwaru ...*' ('*As when in the heat of day ...*')
1. Fonotipia 62289 (ca 1910) — HRS 2002 (before 1925) = Scala (USA) SC 816 = Eterna (USA) 711 = Belcantodisc (England) EB 1 (ca 1954): Giuseppe Anselmi — tenor, with piano accompaniment.
2. His Master's Voice AM 807 (1928): Stanisław Gruszczyński — tenor, the Narodní Divadlo Orchestra in Prague.
3. Syrena-Electro 3378 (ca 1930): Mieczysław Salecki — tenor, Ludwik Urstein — piano.
4. Odeon 271252 (1936): Janusz Popławski — tenor, orchestra, cond. by Stanisław Nawrot.
5. Muza 1224 (1948): Janusz Popławski — tenor, symphony orchestra, cond. by Olgierd Straszyński.
6. Muza XL 0170 (1963): Bogdan Paprocki — tenor, National Philharmonic Orchestra, cond. by Jerzy Semkow.
7. Muza XL 0502 (1969): Stanisław Romański — tenor, Poznań State Opera orchestra, cond. by Edwin Kowalski.
8. Muza SXL 0972 (1975): Wiesław Ochman — tenor, Polish Radio and Television Orchestra in Warsaw, cond. by Zdzisław Górzyński.

Sonata in e-flat minor for piano, Op. 21
1. Muza XL 0570 (1970): Andrzej Stefański — piano.

Variations and Fugue in e-flat minor, Op. 23
1. Muza XL 0570 (1970): Andrzej Stefański — piano.

Symphony in b-minor, Op. 24 '*Polonia*'
1. Muza SXL 0968 (1974): Orchestra of Pomeranian Philharmonic of I. J. Paderewski in Bydgoszcz, cond. by Bohdan Wodiczko.

Repertoire

(compiled by Małgorzata Perkowska)

JOHANN SEBASTIAN BACH
Chromatic Fantasy and Fugue
Gigue (?)

LUDWIG VAN BEETHOVEN
Concerto in E-flat major, Op. 73
Sonata in C-major, Op. 2, No. 3
Sonata quasi fantasia in E-flat major, Op. 27, No. 1
Sonata quasi fantasia in c-sharp minor, Op. 27, No. 2 (*Moonlight*)
Sonata in D-major, Op. 28 (*Pastorale*)
Sonata in d-minor, Op. 31, No. 2
Sonata in E-flat major, Op. 31, No. 3
Sonata in C-major, Op. 53 (*Waldstein*)
Sonata in F-major, Op. 54
Sonata in f-minor, Op. 57 (*Appassionata*)
Sonata in A-major, Op. 101
Sonata in E-major, Op. 109
Sonata in A-flat major, Op. 110
Sonata in c-minor, Op. 111
Trio in B-flat major, Op. 97
32 Variations in c-minor
Violin Sonata in D-major, Op. 12, No. 1

JOHANNES BRAHMS
Capriccio
Hungarian Dances Nos. 1, 6, 7
Intermezzo
Piano Quartet in A-major, Op. 26
Piano Quintet in f-minor, Op. 34
Variations and Fugue on a Theme of Handel, Op. 24
Variations on a Theme of Paganini, Op. 35

CAMILLE CHEVILLARD
Thème et variations, Op. 5

FREDERIC CHOPIN
Ballade in g-minor, Op. 23
Ballade in F-major, Op. 38
Ballade in A-flat major, Op. 47
Ballade in f-minor, Op. 52

Barcarolle in F-sharp major, Op. 60
Berceuse in D-flat major, Op. 57
Concerto in e-minor, Op. 11
Concerto in f-minor, Op. 21
Études, Op. 10, Nos. 3, 4, 5, 7, 10, 12
Études, Op. 25, Nos. 1, 2, 3, 6, 7, 8, 9, 10
Fantasy in f-minor, Op. 49
Funeral March in c-minor, Op. 72
Impromptu in F-sharp major, Op. 36
Mazurka in a-minor, Op. 17, No. 3
Mazurka in b-flat minor, Op. 24, No. 4
Mazurka in b-minor, Op. 33, No. 4
Mazurka in G-major, Op. 50, No. 1
Mazurka in C-major, Op. 56, No. 2
Mazurka in A-flat major, Op. 59, No. 2
Mazurka in f-sharp minor, Op. 59, No. 3
Nocturne in F-major, Op. 15, No. 1
Nocturne in F-sharp major, Op. 15, No. 2
Nocturne in D-flat major, Op. 27, No. 2
Nocturne in B-major, Op. 32, No. 1
Nocturne in g-minor, Op. 37, No. 1
Nocturne in G-major, Op. 37, No. 2
Nocturne in c-minor, Op. 48, No. 1
Nocturne in B-major, Op. 62, No. 1
Nocturne in E-major, Op. 62, No. 2
Polonaise brillante, Op. 3 (violin and piano)
Grande Polonaise brillante in E-flat major, Op. 22
Polonaise in e-flat minor, Op. 26, No. 2
Polonaise in A-major, Op. 40, No.1
Polonaise in f-sharp minor, Op. 44
Polonaise in A-flat major, Op. 53
Polonaise-fantaisie in A-flat major, Op. 61
Preludes, Op. 28, Nos. 1, 7, 16, 17, 21, 24
Scherzo in b-minor, Op. 20
Scherzo in b-flat minor, Op. 31
Scherzo in c-sharp minor, Op. 39
Sonata in b-flat minor, Op. 35
Sonata in b-minor, Op. 58
Grande Valse brillante in E-flat major, Op. 18
Waltz in A-flat major, Op. 34, No. 1
Waltz in a-minor, Op. 34, No. 2

Waltz in A-flat major, Op. 42
Waltz in D-flat major, Op. 64, No. 1
Waltz in c-sharp minor, Op. 64, No. 2

FRANÇOIS COUPERIN
La Bandoline
Le Carillon de Cythère

FREDERIC COWEN
Concertstück

LOUIS CLAUDE DAQUIN
Le Coucou

LÉO DELIBES
Rigaudon

CLAUDE DEBUSSY
Images:
Reflets dans l'eau
Preludes:
Danseuses de Delphes
Minstrels
Le Vent dans la plaine
Voiles

LOUIS DIÉMER
3me Orientale

ALPHONSE VICTOR DUVERNOY
Intermedium

GABRIEL FAURÉ
Barcarolle
Romance sans paroles

JOHN FIELD
Nocturnes

ARTHUR W. FOOTE
Caprice

BENJAMIN GODARD
Polonaise

WITOLD GÓRSKI
Berceuse for violin and piano

EDVARD GRIEG
Concerto in a-minor, Op. 16

GEORGE FREDERIC HANDEL
Harmonius Blacksmith
Suite in d-minor

JOSEPH HAYDN
Variations in f-minor (Andante con variazioni)
Andante varié in f-minor

ADOLF HENSELT
Étude

C. JOHNSS
Valse

THEODOR LESCHETIZKY
Canzonetta toscana
Mazurka
Menuetto capriccioso
Tarantella

FRANZ LISZT
Concerto in E-flat major
Études de Concert
Étude *Ricordanza*
Fantasie über ungarischen Volksweisen
Hungarian Rhapsodies: Nos. 1, 2, 6, 10, 12, 13
Polonaise in E-major No. 2
Sonata in b-flat minor
Spanish Rhapsody
Valse impromptu
Waldesrauschen

Transcriptions:
J. S. Bach
Fantasia and Fugue in a-minor
Fantasia and Fugue in g-minor
Prelude and Fugue in a-minor
F. Chopin
Six Polish Songs
F. Mendelssohn-Bartholdy
Wedding March and *Dance of Elves* from
   Midsummer Night's Dream
W. A. Mozart
Fantasia on *Don Juan*
N. Paganini
La Campanella
F. Schubert
Au bord d'une source
Barcarolle *Auf dem Wasser zu singen*
Divertissement a l'hongroise
Erlkönig
Hungarian March

Serenade *Hark, Hark, the Lark*
Soirée de Vienne
R. Wagner
Fileuse
Isolde's Love-Death
Spinning Song

HENRY CHARLES LITOLFF
Scherzo from Concerto in d-minor

DANIEL G. MASON
Caprice *Spring Dawn*

FELIX MENDELSSOHN-BARTHOLDY
Songs without Words: Op. 19, No. 3, Op. 53,
    No. 4, Op. 62, Nos. 1, 5, Op. 67, No. 4
Prelude and Fugue in e-minor
Variations sérieuses in d-minor, Op. 54

G. P. MOORE
Étude pathétique

MORITZ MOSZKOWSKI
Barcarolle

WOLFGANG AMADEUS MOZART
Rondo in a-minor
Sonata in A-major

ZYGMUNT NOSKOWSKI
Krakowiak

IGNACY JAN PADEREWSKI
Album de mai, Op. 10
Chants du voyageur, Op. 8, Nos. 2, 3
Concerto in a-minor
Humoresques de concert, Op. 14
Miscellanea, Op. 16
Polish Fantasy, Op. 19
Romance from Suite in E-flat major
Sonata, Op. 13 (violin and piano)
Sonata, Op. 21 (piano)
Tatra Album, Op. 12
Toccata (*Dans le désert*), Op. 15
Trois morceaux, Op. 2
Variations and Fugue in a-minor, Op. 11
Variations and Fugue in e-flat minor, Op. 23

A. PÉRILHOU
Fantasia for piano and orchestra
Fugue sur le motif des Pompiers de Nanterre

GABRIEL PIERNÉ
Sérénade à Colombine

SERGEY RACHMANINOFF
Preludes Op. 12

JOSEPH JOACHIM RAFF
Suite for violin and piano, Op. 210
Valse impromptu

ADOLPH RIES
Romance

ANTON RUBINSTEIN
Barcarolle in a-minor, from Op. 93
Barcarolle in f-minor, Op. 30
Concerto No. 4 in d-minor, Op. 70
Étude
La mélancolie, from Op. 51
Mazurka in D-major
Prelude in a-minor
Romance
Trio in B-major
Valse Caprice in E-flat major, from Op. 118

ANTONI RUTKOWSKI
Polonaise

CAMILLE SAINT-SAËNS
Concerto No. 4 in c-minor, Op. 44
Polonaise for two pianos, Op. 77
Romance

DOMENICO SCARLATTI
Capriccio
Pastorale
Sonata

ERNEST SCHELLING
Concerto No. 2
Nocturne à Raguse

FRANZ SCHUBERT
Impromptus
March
Menuet
Moments musicaux, Op. 94
Trio in B-flat major, Op. 99
Variations

ROBERT SCHUMANN
Carnaval, Op. 9
Concerto in a-minor, Op. 54
Études symphoniques, Op. 13
Fantasia in C-major, Op. 17
Fantasiestücke, Op. 12
Faschingsschwank aus Wien, Op. 26
Nachtstücke, Op. 23
Papillons, Op. 2
Sonata in f-sharp minor, Op. 11
Studies after Paganini, Op. 10
Study, Op. 3, No. 2 (after Paganini)
Toccata in C-major, Op. 7
Waldszenen, Op. 82,
No. 7: *Vogel als Prophet*

GIOVANNI SGAMBATI
Gavotte, Op. 9

ZYGMUNT STOJOWSKI
Chant d'amour
Sérénade
By the Brookside

J. STRAUSS —CARL TAUSIG
Valse caprice *Man lebt nur einmal*

KAROL SZYMANOWSKI
Study in b-minor, Op. 4, No. 3

FRANCIS THOMÉ
Chanson du Rouet

PETER TCHAIKOVSKY — PAUL PABST
Paraphrase on *Eugène Onegin*

CARL MARIA VON WEBER
Momento capriccioso, Op. 12
Sonata

HENRYK WIENIAWSKI
Mazurka for violin and piano

CH. M. WINDOR
Zanetto

ALEKSANDER ZARZYCKI
En valsant

WŁADYSŁAW ŻELEŃSKI
Sonata for violin and piano

Index of Names

187

About the Publisher...

The Kościuszko Foundation, an American center for Polish culture, is a non-profit cultural and educational institution dedicated to the promotion of a better knowledge of Polish contributions to world civilization in general and to America in particular. It does so through an exchange of scholars and exhibits between the United States and Poland, through scholarships to needy and deserving students of Polish background, through the publication of books, the organization of lectures, programs, concerts and exhibits. These diverse activities promote a more secure knowledge of Polish heritage among Americans of Polish descent and thus develop that sense of pride in the accomplishments of their ancestors which is basic to an appreciation of their own American heritage. The Foundation's headquarters are at 15 East 65th Street, New York, New York 10021.

The illustrative materials reproduced in the present album come from the collections of the Archives of the Jagiellonian University in Cracow, Archives of Recent Documents in Warsaw, Geographical Institute of the Jagiellonian University in Cracow, Jagiellonian Library in Cracow, National Philharmonic in Warsaw, PWM-Edition in Cracow, State College of Music in Warsaw, Theatrical Museum in Warsaw, Tytus Chałubiński Museum of the Tatra Region in Zakopane and from the private collections of Janina Byszewska of Cracow, Wiktoryna Kostkowa of Cracow, Zofia Krajewska of Krynica, Kazimiera Szpinalska of Warsaw, Henryk Sztompka of Cracow, and others. Photographs: Władysław Dulęba.